THE BEST
MEDITATIONS
ON THE PLANET

THE BEST
MEDITATIONS
ON THE PLANET

100 TECHNIQUES TO BEAT STRESS,
IMPROVE HEALTH, AND CREATE HAPPINESS—
IN JUST MINUTES PER DAY

DR. MARTIN HART AND SKYE ALEXANDER

FAIR WINDS
PRESS
BEVERLY, MASSACHUSETTS

© 2011 Fair Winds Press
Text © 2011 Martin Hart and Skye Alexander

First published in the USA in 2011 by
Fair Winds Press, a member of
Quayside Publishing Group
100 Cummings Center
Suite 406-L
Beverly, MA 01915-6101
www.fairwindspress.com

15 14 13   3 4 5

ISBN: 978-1-59233-459-9

Library of Congress Cataloging-in-Publication Data

Hart, Martin.
The best meditations on the planet : / 120 techniques to beat stress, improve health, and create happiness in just
minutes per day / Martin Hart and Skye Alexander.
    p. cm.
Includes bibliographical references and index.
ISBN-13: 978-1-59233-459-9 (alk. paper)
ISBN-10: 1-59233-459-8 (alk. paper)
1. Stress (Psychology) 2. Meditation. 3. Happiness. I. Alexander, Skye. II. Title.

BF575.S75H3967 2011
158.1'2--dc22

2010047043

Cover and book design by Debbie Berne Design
Photography by istockphoto.com 12, 26, 28, 45, 48, 61, 63, 65, 66, 95, 118, 124, 133, 140, 148, 151, 158, 160, 163,
173, 175, 180, 182, 191, 198, 207, 215, 218; Thinkstock.com 31, 32, 69, 83, 93, 99, 111, 121, 123, 138, 145, 153, 177,
193, 201, 202, 205, 212; Fotolia 38, 75, 86, 102; Alamy 170; Jack Deutsch from *Reflexology Card Deck* (Fair Winds
Press, 2008) 104

Printed and bound in China

*The information in this book is for educational purposes only. It is not intended to replace the advice of a physician
or medical practitioner. Please see your health-care provider before beginning any new health program.*

To my kids at Masconomet Regional, who teach me every day how to laugh and love, and to my fellow staff members, who teach me how to have lunch.

—M.H.

To Domino —S.A.

Go into yourself and see how deep the place is from which your life flows.

—Rainer Maria Rilke

CONTENTS

DON'T JUST DO SOMETHING . . . SIT THERE

East Meets West

Few Westerners knew much about meditation until 1959, when the Indian teacher Maharishi Mahesh Yogi introduced Transcendental Meditation (TM) to the United States. Based in the Vedic tradition, TM uses a mantra to induce relaxation and transcend thinking. Meditation's popularity grew throughout the 1960s, due in part to the influence of the Beatles, who had studied with Maharishi in India. During the next fifty years, Maharishi trained forty thousand teachers, who took the TM technique to more than five million people worldwide. Martin was one of those teachers.

In 1980, Martin traveled to India, where he spent a year instructing more than 1,500 people in the Transcendental Meditation technique, ranging from schoolchildren to scientists to top executives in some of Asia's largest corporations, including the chief medical officer of India's largest bank—Deepak Chopra's sister—and her two sons. Martin has since branched out into other areas and has developed a unique counseling system called ASAT™ C.O.R.E. Counseling. To date he has trained more than 1,700 ASAT™ C.O.R.E counselors through the auspices of the American Society of Alternative Therapists (ASAT™), which he founded in 1990. Combining meditation with a specific counseling approach to address hidden blockages and templates, these counselors report remarkable results with clients from all walks of life.

In the latter half of the twentieth century, other forms of meditation spread through the West as well. Insight or mindfulness meditation, for instance, brings you into a deep awareness of the present moment so you can fully experience the here and now. Visualization and guided imagery use mental pictures to encourage body-mind relaxation or to generate specific results. Yoga combines postures (asanas) and breathing to shift awareness into a meditative state. More than twenty million Americans—one in eleven—now meditate regularly. In this book, we present 100 different meditations designed for a wide range of objectives, from lowering blood pressure to improving athletic performance to increasing your IQ.

A CURE FOR WHAT AILS YOU

As meditation's popularity expanded, so did research to investigate its effects on the mind and body—and its potential to aid all sorts of physical, mental, emotional, and societal ills. During the past four decades, more than six hundred studies conducted at 250 universities and medical schools worldwide have verified meditation's efficacy. More than 350 scientific and medical journals have published research showing the benefits of meditation for conditions including diabetes, coronary disease, cancer, chronic pain, and more. Most of the research to date has centered on TM, mindfulness (insight) meditation, or a combination of techniques. In this book, we present some of the amazing results of these studies.

In the United States, the National Institutes of Health has provided more than $24 million in grants to investigate the health benefits of meditation. Meditation programs are available at more than 240 hospitals and medical facilities. The University of Massachusetts Medical School's Center for Mindfulness in Medicine, Health Care, and Society, which grew out of the Stress Reduction Clinic founded more than thirty years ago by Jon Kabat-Zinn, PhD, is the oldest and largest academic medical center–based stress reduction program in the world. It pioneered the integration of meditation and other mindfulness-based approaches into mainstream medicine and served as the model for more than 200 medical centers in the United States and other countries.

Today's researchers at major universities and medical facilities worldwide continue to discover new ways to utilize meditation's therapeutic powers, from promoting stem cell growth to increasing brain size. We may have just begun to tap meditation's abilities to heal body, mind, and spirit.

MEDITATION GOES MAINSTREAM

Following his training with Maharishi, Martin traveled to India in 1980, where he was impressed with how eagerly the heads of India's major corporations pursued meditation training. From top physicists at the Bhabha Atomic Research Center in Bombay (Mumbai) to corporate leaders at Tata Motors and Mahindra and Mahindra, Ltd., hundreds of people enthusiastically sought meditation as a means to finding their own inner reservoirs of peace and well-being. The ironic thing was that a Westerner reconnected them to a practice deeply rooted in their own culture.

Today, an increasing number of businesses offer meditation classes for their employees, including companies such as Apple Computer, Yahoo, Google, Raytheon, McKinsey & Company, Deutsche Bank, AOL Time Warner, and Hughes Aircraft.

As employee stress mounts due to economic challenges and increased work demands, meditation seems the logical answer for companies seeking to rein in costs, boost productivity, and keep good employees happy. Stress-related problems cost companies about $200 billion a year, according to the National Institute for Occupational Safety & Health. "If businesses were clever," says Harvard Medical School's Herbert Benson, MD, best-selling author of *The Relaxation Response*, "what they would do is simply put time aside [and have] a quiet room for people to carry out a meditative behavior of their choice."

In addition to businesses, public schools in the U.S. are beginning to teach meditation to children and teens. A study by the Medical College of Georgia in 2003 found that meditation helped students lower stress, get better grades, and improve their interpersonal relationships.

Meditation could have a positive impact on crime, too. When 1,350 inmates at six Massachusetts prisons practiced meditation, hostility diminished and their self-esteem improved.

Even the U.S. military is exploring meditation as a way to treat post-traumatic stress disorder and traumatic brain injury. The Defense Department spent $5 million in 2008 researching meditation and other complementary healing modalities.

Clearly, meditation has moved out of the ashram and into the mainstream. As clinical research and personal experience show, meditation's benefits are diverse, vast, and readily available to everyone who seeks them. All it takes is a few minutes a day and a desire to enjoy a healthier, happier life.

We hope the meditations offered in this book will assist you in that pursuit.

WHAT MEDITATION CAN DO FOR YOU

Meditation only takes a short period of time each day, costs absolutely nothing, requires no special equipment or accoutrements, and can be done successfully by anyone, anywhere, anytime. Meditation could be the single most valuable tool we have available to heal ourselves and our planet.

During the past two decades, hundreds of scientific studies have been conducted at more than 250 universities and research facilities internationally to examine meditation's efficacy. Although devotees of the practice may assert that meditation can do everything from create world peace to make you a better lover, clinical research clearly shows that meditation's benefits are substantial and far-reaching. Here are just some of the amazing results top scientific and medical researchers have linked to meditation:

- Meditation lowers blood pressure and decreases the risk of heart attack and stroke.
- Meditation boosts intelligence and academic performance.
- Meditation stimulates stem cell growth.
- Meditation saves companies money by reducing employee absenteeism.
- Meditation enhances athletic performance.
- Meditation decreases substance abuse.
- Meditation relieves depression and anxiety.
- Meditation aids weight loss.
- Meditation eases chronic pain.
- Meditation reduces hyperactivity in children.
- Meditation improves memory in the elderly.
- Meditation increases longevity.
- Meditation deters crime.

How Meditation Works

When you meditate, you stop thinking about work, relationships, finances, and daily chores, and become present in the moment. Mental chatter ceases temporarily and you experience a state of relaxation in both mind and body.

The changes you experience can actually be measured physically. During meditation, your heart rate and respiration slow. Brain wave frequencies slow from the usual 13 to 30 cycles per second (the beta, or active, outwardly focused, level of consciousness) to 8 to 13 cps (the alpha level, a more inwardly focused, expanded state of awareness). Brain wave activity also shifts from the right frontal cortex to the left. Richard J. Davidson, PhD, a researcher and neuroscientist at the University of Wisconsin, has been studying meditation's effects for more than two decades. When he examined the brains of Buddhist monks to see how meditation affected their neural physiology, he discovered the left frontal cortex (the part of the brain linked to happiness) was more active in the monks than in people who didn't meditate.

During meditation, the brain also steps up production of endorphins, the proteins that enhance positive feelings. According to a recent clinical trial of 97,000 subjects conducted by the Women's Health Initiative, positive, optimistic people enjoy longer, healthier lives than their negative, pessimistic peers.

Using modern brain-scanning technology, researchers have discovered that meditation produces long-term physiological changes as well. A UCLA study, led by neuroscientist Eileen Luders, PhD, demonstrated that meditation actually increases the size of the brain. The study's results, released in 2009, showed that the areas of the brain associated with attention, focus, and positive emotions were larger in people who meditate regularly than in non-meditators. Meditation causes changes in cell metabolism, too, according to another study performed at the Benson-Henry Institute for Mind Body Medicine at Massachusetts General Hospital and reported in *Medical News Today* in 2008. The changes, explained Dr. Jeffery Dusek, co-lead author of the study, were the opposite of those induced by posttraumatic stress disorder.

These and other clinical studies reveal that meditation strengthens the part of the brain linked with positive emotions while counteracting the destructive impact of stress and anxiety. Indeed, stress reduction may be the key to meditation's beneficial effects on health. At least 60 percent of all doctor visits are due to stress-related problems. "It's hard to think of an illness in which stress and mood don't figure," points out Charles L. Raison, MD, clinical director of the Mind-Body Program at Emory University School of Medicine in Atlanta.

The brain wave changes induced by meditation also boost stem cell production, enhancing the body's ability to regenerate and repair itself. Leading stem cell researcher Doris Taylor, PhD, director of the Center for Cardiovascular Repair at the University of Minnesota, measured the blood of Matthieu Ricard, French philosopher and author of the book *Happiness*, before and after meditation. The result after only fifteen minutes of meditation "was a huge increase in the number of positive stem cells in [his] blood."

But you needn't be a Buddhist monk or a "meditation marathoner" to reap the rewards of meditation. Both Richard Davidson, PhD, director of the Lab for Affective Neuroscience at the University of Wisconsin–Madison, and Sara Lazar, PhD, a neuroscientist at Beth Israel Deaconess Medical Center, have studied meditation's effects on ordinary, middle-class Americans. "What we found out," says Davidson, "is that after a short time meditating, meditation had profound effects not just on how they felt but on their brains and bodies."

For twenty-first-century Westerners struggling to cope with ever-increasing stress in their professional and personal lives, turning to this ancient Eastern practice may be the answer to enjoying happier, healthier, longer lives.

Handling Resistances

The three most common obstacles to meditation are the following:

- Falling asleep during meditation
- Too many thoughts
- Procrastination

All these are resistances, and all come from one source: fear. Here's an example of how resistance works. Let's say you want to leave an unhappy relationship. But you're afraid of being alone, or fear you won't be able to support yourself financially, or believe the end of a relationship means you're a failure. Your resistance kicks in. You procrastinate. You distract yourself with work or other activities. You tune out (figuratively fall asleep). Meditation lets you become aware of your feelings and motivations—and your resistance—so you can take responsibility for acting on that awareness.

Meditation is the doorway to the vast power of the mind. Within you resides the ability to change what you don't like about your life and to create what you desire instead. You may not be in touch with this ability all the time. But you've undoubtedly tapped it—drawing on your inner resources and power—at times in your life when you really needed to. You may even have realized, much to your surprise, that you were capable of more than you thought possible. However, most of us have some distorted, fear-based perceptions concerning power. We tend to think of it as "power over," or domination, or violence. This produces inner templates of fear.

During meditation, old templates you may have about "power" will surface to block the meditation, in the form of resistance. As humans, we all deal with fear in one or a combination of four ways: denial, discounting, defense, and distraction. When we fall asleep during meditation, we're using the mechanisms of defense or distraction. When we have too many thoughts and our minds wander all over the place, we're experiencing another form of distraction. Procrastination is a distraction, too.

Instead of trying to "overcome" resistances to fear, which would perpetuate the distorted ideas linking power with aggression, we would be better served by acknowledging our fear, recognizing where it is coming from, attending to it, and releasing it. The following suggestions can help you work with resistance:

FALLING ASLEEP

- Before meditating, close your eyes and, as best you can, become still. In whatever state of calmness you feel, mentally reassure your frightened "younger selves" (the inner children in which the fear resides) that everything will be fine; you (the adult) are here, won't leave, and will keep them safe.
- Sit instead of lying down to meditate. If that doesn't work, try standing against a wall while holding on to a chair. It might seem strange at first, but it's hard to fall asleep in a standing position.

TOO MANY THOUGHTS

- Close your eyes and, as best you can, become still. In whatever state of calmness you feel, mentally reassure your frightened "younger selves" that everything will be fine; you (the adult) are here, won't leave, and will keep them safe.
- Pay attention to the resistance you experience. Be honest with yourself. Write your feelings down in your meditation journal.
- Do not force yourself to sit and meditate. Instead, try doing one of the active "waking" meditations, such as taking a walk in nature.
- Ask your Higher Self to heal the resistance and lift it from you while you meditate. (This should not be a substitute for processing through your fear after the meditation is over.)

PROCRASTINATION

- If you're too busy to meditate, you're too busy.
- Discipline yourself. Establish a time to meditate and stick to it. Make meditation part of your daily routine.
- Remove distractions. Turn off the TV. Spend less time at the computer.
- Ask your Higher Self to heal the resistances.

Everything is a product of your intention and what you give attention to. If you truly want to meditate and devote your attention to it, the resistance will be but a brief nuisance. Ask your Higher Self for help—the answer will always be "yes."

MISCONCEPTIONS ABOUT MEDITATION

Before we begin our adventure into the wondrous world of meditation, let's clear the air of some widely held misconceptions surrounding it.

Meditation is for followers of Eastern religions who live in ashrams. The belief that meditative practices are the sole domain of an esoteric few who commit themselves to untold years sitting in isolated caves or sequestered in rarefied ashrams is false. Although some people seek "enlightenment" in this manner, that is a choice, not a requirement. The truth is that meditation belongs to all of us. Everyone can meditate and everyone can attain unlimited benefits from its practice. You can meditate regardless of your physical, mental, or emotional condition. Your age, race, gender, and nationality don't matter. You do not need to be an ascetic, a monk, or a sadhu (ascetic) to meditate. Oprah meditates. So do Congressman Tim Ryan, Wall Street whiz Walter Zimmermann, and bond-fund king William H. Gross. You can choose to meditate as part of a religious practice—and most of the world's major religions do advocate meditation in one form or another—but meditation itself is a "human" experience, not a "religious" one.

Meditation is difficult and takes years to learn. The only difficulty comes from someone's resistance to meditation and its success. Meditation is a pleasurable and enjoyable experience, not a Bataan Death March for the mind. The belief that meditation's benefits come only after years of effort is erroneous. Every time you sit in meditation you achieve results: some may be what you expect; others, not. Virtually anyone can meditate. Focus, awareness, and relaxation do improve with practice. Although there is no such thing as a "magic bullet" that will cure every problem, meditation always works—but the results are not "quick fixes."

For example, you may meditate to achieve a slimmer, healthier body. Meditation will help make you aware of the unconscious eating behaviors that sabotage you; it will also give you the confidence to stick to your diet and exercise regimen. Some evidence suggests that meditation even boosts metabolism. However, you can't meditate for ten minutes and wake up the next day ten pounds lighter. Meditation will, in time, produce the results you seek—or reveal your resistance to realizing those results.

You need a lot of spare time to meditate. Although some people may choose to meditate for extended periods of time, and some meditations take longer than others, you'll notice benefits even if you spend only ten minutes a day meditating. Most of the meditations in this book can be done in a half hour or less; some require only a few minutes.

You Always Get What You Want (Although It May Not Be What You Ask For)

Meditation is not a quick fix or a "magic bullet." It can't make choices for you or override the parts of you that will prevent, if left unaddressed, your success. Meditation is extremely powerful, but never more powerful than your hidden intentions, fears, or limiting beliefs from your past that you haven't yet faced and released. These hidden parts of yourself keep you trapped in the past and ensure failure. For example, if you fear you are unlovable and your unconscious intention is to shield yourself from rejection, then it doesn't matter how many singles events you attend—you aren't likely to create a satisfying relationship. Meditation will help bring these hidden intentions, fears, and beliefs to your attention so you can heal and release them. In *Molecules of Emotion*, Candace Pert, PhD, writes, "Meditation . . . allows us, even without conscious awareness, to release emotions that are stuck in modes that subvert a healthy mind-body flow of biochemicals."

Many healing traditions, such as Ayurvedic medicine and homeopathy, assert that all discomfort and disease have their source in the unconscious, and eventually emerge into consciousness or our four-square reality as some form of mental, emotional, or physical ailment or imbalance. Listening to the "voice" of the unconscious and directing healing to it can—and does—produce profound and amazing results.

How can you communicate with your unconscious? The unconscious doesn't speak to us in English, French, Spanish, or any other human tongue—it uses the language of myth, metaphor, archetype, and symbol, according to Swiss analyst Carl Jung. That's why meditations often include imagery to convey intentions. Meditations that communicate in this language direct your healing intention to the "source" (the unconscious) in a way that no conscious method, analytical approach, or technological device can.

More important, meditation invites unconscious issues to surface so you can address them consciously. This is the principal healing benefit of meditation. Your experiences during and after meditation are the unconscious mind's response to what you've asked of it. If you ask it to manifest something—health, prosperity, career success, or a relationship—the unconscious will first "bring up" your resistances to receiving what you've requested.

Meditation provides a doorway between your conscious, subconscious, and unconscious minds. Imagination, meditation's principal tool, is, in fact, the bridge between your inner and outer worlds. The unconscious mind's awareness is infinite. The conscious mind's awareness is finite. The conscious mind, however, possesses an important faculty the unconscious lacks: the ability to make choices. When the two work together, your choices and actions become more creative, more intelligent, more effective, and more fulfilling. In other words, when you consciously make choices based on what your subconscious and unconscious present to you, you become more empowered.

Here's an analogy: The staff of a corporation (the unconscious) powers the corporation as a whole. The CEO (the conscious mind) directs the corporation's decision making. The CEO's management team (meditation) brings to the CEO information relevant to the decision-making process. You are the CEO of your life. Nothing changes until you do. What you secretly want, you always get.

Sometimes what you want isn't what you've consciously asked for, however. Here's an example: A man asks to be cured of cancer, but he finds that the illness is bringing him much-wanted attention. Although he wants to be free of the disease, he unconsciously craves the attention more. The cancer will remain as long as it serves him. If he changes his reliance on what the cancer is providing him (i.e., attention), there will be no need for the disease to remain. Whatever healing procedure, technique, or regimen he chooses will now have a chance to work.

Some of the meditations in this book are designed specifically to help you process unconscious intentions, fears, agendas, and so on. The work you do on yourself before and after the meditation involves discipline, sincerity, and honesty. We recommend working with the following meditation: "Unblock Your Creativity" (part 10) and "Attract Whatever You Desire—While You Sleep" (part 9). If you approach this work with commitment, if you can feel and listen to what your meditations bring up for you and choose to act on them, the results will be nothing less than miraculous. Remember, however, that meditation in and of itself does not change your life. You change your life.

Prepare to Meditate

Meditating is easy. It does not involve complicated rituals or specially designed environments.

MEDITATION ACCOMPLISHES THREE THINGS

- It attracts things into your life.

- It removes things from your life.

- It makes you aware of your resistance to allowing the first two to happen.

You don't need any tools or accoutrements. You don't have to sit in funny positions or burn incense (unless you want to). All you need is a comfortable place to sit or lie down. You can meditate any time of the day or night, at home or work, indoors or outside, alone or with other people. Give yourself a little bit of quiet, private time. Twenty-five to forty minutes a day is ideal, but if in the beginning you can only devote ten minutes to meditation, that's fine. You'll still see results. The following suggestions will help make the experience go more smoothly for you.

AVOID DISTURBANCES

Turn off the phone; put a "do not disturb" sign on the door; meditate before other family members arrive home; meditate when the baby is napping; meditate at times when there's little or no outside noise; and so on.

WHAT IF I CAN'T VISUALIZE?

You've probably heard the terms *creative visualization* and *guided imagery* in connection with meditation. One of the problems with these terms is they imply that you must "see" mentally what you're experiencing internally. This is not so.

Just as our physical senses make our outer world real to us, so too do our inner senses make our inner world real. Although most of us have five physical senses, we do not use them equally. Some senses are stronger or weaker than others. For some people, taste is the strongest physical sense. For others it's hearing, touch, smell, or sight.

In meditation, the same holds true. Some of our inner senses are not as developed as others. Maybe you find it hard to visualize, yet you can hear, smell, touch, or even taste the inner experience. That's fine. Not being able to visualize in meditation does not limit or detract from the experience or its benefits. The most important experience you have when meditating is the experience of *whatever it is you feel*.

Most people who claim they cannot internally visualize actually can visualize very well. The static caused by their resistance to meditation—and more particularly, to the potential benefits they may derive from meditation—accounts for their lack of "inner seeing." Face your resistances as a separate issue; if you process through them using the methods described in this book, you'll be surprised at how well you can visualize.

A VISUALIZATION "TEST"

Close your eyes and relax in whatever way is comfortable for you. Take a deep breath and exhale. Do this two more times. Sit quietly for a few moments.

1 } Now, imagine the outside of your house or apartment. Is it a single- or multi-story structure? What color is the building? What material is it made of?

2 } Do trees or bushes grow in front?

3 } What do you notice (from your memory) of its exterior appearance? Does it have a porch? What type of windows?

4 } Now, change the image you see. Change its color. If the building is white, make it blue. If there are no trees in the yard, add one or two. If lots of trees grow there, imagine the place without trees.

5 } In your memory, add or take away various features from the building. You can change anything you like.

6 } When you feel you've finished making changes, open your eyes.

If you were able to visualize changes to your home in this little exercise, guess what? *You can visualize.*

BE SPECIFIC ABOUT WHAT YOU WANT FROM THE MEDITATION

Instead of saying "I want to feel better," try "I want to end this headache." Instead of "I want my business to improve," think "I want twelve more sales this week." Stay within your range of belief. Don't program your mind beyond what you feel is possible. Your unconscious cannot be fooled—it will know you're just "playing around."

MEDITATE AT A TIME THAT'S BEST FOR YOU

Meditation in the morning can affect the entire day in wonderful ways. Meditating when you get home from work or school is a good idea, too, and lets you release the stress of the day. Meditating before going to bed can be great, as long as you don't fall asleep. (If you do, try sitting up to meditate.) Meditating before bed programs the unconscious mind to work with your intention during the night.

COMFORT IS IMPORTANT

Choose a place to sit or lie down where you feel safe and comfortable. Wear clothing that doesn't bind or restrict you.

DON'T MEDITATE IMMEDIATELY AFTER EATING A LARGE MEAL

The body's act of metabolizing food increases the mind's activity, so you'll get more thoughts (mental noise) during the meditation.

DON'T MEDITATE IF YOU FEEL DESPERATE

Desperation blocks meditation. Close your eyes. Take a few slow, deep breaths. As you inhale, feel yourself beginning to relax; as you exhale, let the desperation go. Ask your Higher Self to lift it from you. (We'll talk more about your Higher Self in just a bit.) When you feel free, meditate.

MEDITATING WITH OTHER PEOPLE CAN BE A POWERFUL EXPERIENCE

When you combine your meditation with that of other people who are in the same "space" as you are, the results become exponentially greater. Remember to be respectful to the others in the room and insist that they be respectful of you. This is not a time for talking, giggling, or making any other type of noise.

ALLOW SOME TIME AFTER MEDITATION BEFORE RESUMING ACTIVITY

If possible, lie down for a bit after meditating. The transition from a state of meditation to one of activity should always be slow and comfortable, even if you feel the meditation was not that "deep." Don't rush.

MEDITATE DAILY

Above all, choose to meditate every day and stick with it. Meditation's benefits are cumulative. The rewards you reap will increase with dedication and consistency. We recommend meditating once or twice per day, and not more than twice. Too much meditating can be a sign of desperation and, as such, will produce few results. Meditation works; desperation doesn't.

Find Your Safe Place

Every meditation you undertake will begin from a "Safe Place" within you. Your outer circumstance may be chaotic, but *your inner world must be safe.*

Close your eyes and use your imagination to create an inner place of peace and security that's private and tranquil, a place no one can enter unless invited in by you. You can remember a special place from your past, choose a place in your current life, recall one from a photo or movie you've seen—or make it up entirely. What does it look like? Notice the details of your surroundings. Is it by an ocean or high up in the mountains? Are there trees and flowers? Do your senses pick up anything else? Does your Safe Place have a pleasant fragrance? What does the air feel like on your skin? There is no right or wrong. This is a Safe Place created by you, for you. You'll go to this place each time you meditate, and return from it once your inner journey has ended. This Safe Place is one you create—no one should create it for you.

- The Safe Place must be in nature. Do not imagine forts, buildings, castles, public structures, and so on; these suggest to your unconscious that you are in "defense mode," not a spot where you feel safe, relaxed, and at peace.
- Use the same Safe Place to begin every directed inward meditation. Changing from place to place tells the unconscious you are unsure, scattered, insecure, or inconsistent.
- Each time you meditate, notice a little more about this wondrous place you've chosen. Observe its beauty. Remember the saying, "Love pays attention to detail." Maybe you see a plant or shrub you never paid attention to before. What about that rock? Use your inner senses. What fragrances do you smell? What does this place taste like? Reach out and touch things. Listen to the sounds around you.

Before doing any of the directed inward meditations in this book, we recommend that you spend some time—perhaps fifteen to twenty minutes each day for a week—in this Safe Place within yourself. You needn't "see" this place clearly. Perceiving it with any of your inner senses will suffice. The most important thing is to feel its safety and security. Know that you belong here.

Get to Know Your Higher Self

Within each of us is a part that transcends our conscious awareness; in this book we call that part your Higher Self. It is impossible to accurately describe the Higher Self in words or to comprehend it fully. You could think of it as the part of you that is always in communication with Spirit, God, Goddess, Buddha, or something else. The Higher Self is the highest expression of you, or as physics would describe it, a higher resonance of you.

We have all had encounters with the Higher Self, although we may have difficulty expressing this after the fact. You might experience it during times of crisis, when you sense something wiser and more powerful than your ordinary human self protecting and guiding you. Or, you may experience it during times of ecstasy, when you sense a loving and expansive "presence" joyfully celebrating with you. During such times you realize you are not alone, that "someone" is with you.

- Your Higher Self is a part of you, but it's more than you as well.
- Your Higher Self is not physical. It is neither male nor female. Some people experience it as a being of light, but try not to project any expectations onto it.

- Your Higher Self's awareness is greater than that of your conscious self. Working with your Higher Self will enable you to bring more awareness into your daily life.
- Your Higher Self is *not* your guru, mother, father, or oracle—don't ask it to pick the winning horse in the seventh race at San Anita. Communicate with it as you would a beloved and respected friend.

Meditation, in its role as a doorway between the conscious, subconscious, and unconscious, allows you access to unconscious information, as dreams do. The problem is that without a "guide" who's familiar with the boundless terrain and incomprehensible language of the unconscious, and who possesses enough awareness to navigate the unconscious's unfathomable depths, you can get lost when using meditation for healing, insight, and manifestation. No books, gurus, or therapists can help you here, for their conscious awareness is limited, too. There is, however, a solution. We call it "working with your Higher Self."

Many of the meditations in this book can guide you in this practice. We strongly encourage you to work with your Higher Self in the meditations where we've indicated doing so. It will help you navigate the unconscious mind and serve as your counsel. As you work with your Higher Self and experience its love, your life will take on more richness. Spend as much time as you need to develop your connection with your Higher Self. It's important to progress at your own pace.

As you continue meditating, you'll come to know and appreciate your Higher Self more fully. Developing the connection with your Higher Self

CONSCIOUS, SUBCONSCIOUS, AND UNCONSCIOUS MINDS

The conscious mind calibrates and constructs all that you sense outside of yourself.

The subconscious mind holds the myriad beliefs, templates, and instructions you've accumulated as a result of your lifetime experiences. It filters opportunities that present themselves, and either allows them in or rejects them. For example, if at the age of fifteen you placed into your subconscious the instruction "I'll never love like that again," when the opportunity for love presents itself at age forty-two, the subconscious instruction (unless consciously removed) will kick in and sabotage the opportunity.

The unconscious mind transcends the conscious and subconscious, yet it includes these parts as well. Everything is contained in the unconscious. If you liken the conscious mind to planet Earth, the subconscious would be our solar system, and the unconscious would be all possible universes.

TAPE-RECORD A DIRECTED MEDITATION

Some people find that a tape recording of the directed inward meditations makes them more enjoyable and easier to do. Listening to your own voice guiding the meditation is very beneficial. When recording, go slowly. You may wish to record a meditation several times until you achieve a comfortable pace and flow.

can make the experience of meditation—as well as the results you receive from meditation—more powerful and magical. It can change everything and anything in your life.

How to Work with the Meditations in This Book

The meditations contained in this book are versatile. Although we've organized them into specific parts for specific needs, they can be easily adapted to address any need or desire you may have. In part 9, for example, you'll find a meditation called "Use a Crystal to Attract Prosperity," but you can do it attract anything else you want as well. Likewise, you can use the meditation titled "Dialogue with Your Cancer" in part 3 to work with any health issue. Feel free to modify a meditation by simply replacing the book's suggested use with your own intention. We recommend, however,

that you don't alter the meditation's "story" or structure, because these are designed to communicate directly with the unconscious using specific myths, metaphors, archetypes, and symbols the unconscious will comprehend.

If you prefer, you can let your unconscious and Higher Self select a meditation for you. Hold a desire in your mind. See it clearly. See it successfully fulfilled. Feel what having it in your life would be like. Now, open this book, and without looking, point to a page. Do the meditation on that page. Or you can write on flash cards the names of the meditations contained in this book. Shuffle the deck and randomly select a card, then do that meditation. After you've worked with some of the meditations in this book, try creating your own meditation or inner journeying experience. You can also begin a meditation and just let your Higher Self take you where it will. It will be a powerful experience.

You may wish to keep a special "meditation journal" and record what transpired during your meditations. Include everything you experienced sensually—sights, sounds, tactile experiences, tastes, scents. Write the "story" of what happened. Most important, write what you felt. Feel it as you write it. Did anger come up? Anxiety? Serenity? Joy? Write it all down. You could even include a drawing of the meditation. All this helps bring unconscious information to your conscious mind, and eventually into your conscious experience.

Some of the meditations in this book may not resonate with you. Select the ones that do and work with them. Above all, enjoy—no strain, no struggle, no stress; just fun.

THE CHAKRAS

Healing and balancing the chakras is an objective of many holistic healing therapies. *Chakra* is a Sanskrit term meaning wheel. To sensitive individuals who can see them, these nonphysical energy centers resemble spinning wheels located roughly along the spine. The life force travels up the spinal column and energizes these vortices. Each chakra is associated with certain parts of the body. When the chakras become blocked or don't operate properly, illness occurs. Health and happiness result when the life force flows freely and harmoniously through the chakras.

Each chakra corresponds to a color of the visible spectrum and a note of the musical scale; consequently, chromotherapy and sound healing can be particularly effective in chakra work. Eastern healing and spiritual traditions consider these seven main chakras to be most important:

Root chakra—located at the base of the spine, this energy center is associated with the survival instinct and your sense of security. It controls the bones, teeth, spine, rectum, and colon. The root chakra's color is red and its musical note is C.

Sacral chakra—found near the abdomen in the vicinity of the lower back, about a hand's width below the belly button, this chakra is related to creativity and sexuality. The reproductive organs, kidneys, and bladder are influenced by the sacral chakra. Its color is orange and its musical note is D.

Solar plexus chakra—located at the solar plexus, about halfway between your belly button and heart, this chakra is connected with the will and personal power. It controls the stomach, liver, digestive system, spleen, gall bladder, the autonomic nervous system, and the muscles. Its color is yellow and its musical note is E.

Heart chakra—situated near the heart, this chakra regulates the heart, blood circulation, skin, chest, and upper back. The center of love and emotions, its color is green and its musical note is F.

Throat chakra—found at the base of the neck, between the collarbones, this chakra is associated with self-expression and communication. The jaw, neck, voice, upper lungs, and arms are linked to the throat chakra. Its color is blue and its musical note is G.

Brow chakra—located on the forehead between the eyebrows, at the site of the "third eye," this chakra is the center of intuition. It controls the endocrine system, nose, left brain, and left eye. Its color is indigo and its musical note is A.

Crown chakra—situated at the top of the head, the crown chakra is associated with the soul and your connection to the Divine. The central nervous system, cerebrum, right brain, and right eye are controlled by this chakra. Its color is violet and its musical note is B.

An illustration of these chakras can be found on page 65.

(Excerpted from Skye's book *The Care and Feeding of Your Chi*.)

Perhaps the most frequently prescribed healing advice is "Get plenty of rest." Rest and relaxation offer an antidote to stress, which is a major contributor to all types of physical, emotional, and mental health ills. In his best-selling book, *The Relaxation Response*, Herbert Benson, MD, discusses his experiments on meditators. His research established that meditation dramatically lowered heart rate and oxygen consumption—both indicators of deep states of relaxation. Benson concluded that meditation had a very real effect on reducing stress and controlling the fight-or-flight response.

MEDITATIONS FOR
RELAXATION AND
STRESS RELIEF

PRACTICE POLARITY BREATHING TO SLEEP BETTER

Linda E. Carlson, PhD, and her colleagues at the University of Calgary in Calgary, Alberta, conducted an eight-week meditation study involving sixty-three patients (published in 2005 in the *International Journal of Behavioral Medicine*). The researchers found that meditation significantly decreased sleep dysfunction in the study's participants and improved their overall quality of sleep.

Many types of meditation emphasize paying attention to your breath as a way to clear your mind and quiet your body. The following meditation, based on an ancient yogic breathing technique, balances the body's yin (receptive/passive) and yang (assertive/active) energies and produces a calm, tranquil state. Practice this technique every night when you go to bed to help you relax and sleep better.

1 } Lie on your back, with your eyes closed. With your right thumb, gently close off your right nostril. Breathe slowly and deeply through your left nostril. Inhale, letting your breath fill your abdomen first, then your chest. Exhale, expelling air from your chest first, then your abdomen, until all the breath has been released.

2 } Repeat, and continue breathing in this manner for about a minute. Pay attention to your breathing. Notice how your abdomen rises and falls as you inhale and exhale.

3 } Now, with your left thumb, close off your left nostril. Breathe slowly and deeply through your right nostril. Inhale, letting your breath fill your abdomen first, then your chest. Exhale, expelling air from your chest first, then your abdomen, until all the breath has been released.

4 } Repeat, and continue breathing in this manner for about a minute. Keep your attention focused on your breath.

5 } If your mind starts to wander, gently bring it back to your breathing. Feel your breath circulating through your body.

6 } Feel your mind and body gradually relaxing, as your system comes into harmony.

7 } Switch nostrils again and continue. Do this for as long as is comfortable, or until you fall asleep.

RELIEVE COMPUTER-RELATED TENSION

Computers make our lives easier in some ways, but they also add frustration and increase the demand to produce more, faster. Sitting at a computer for hours on end puts pressure on your neck and shoulders as well. Charles L. Raison, MD, clinical director of the Mind-Body Program at Emory University School of Medicine in Atlanta, found in a six-week study that meditation had a positive effect on participants' responses to both physical and emotional stress. This "waking" meditation, or directed, outward form of meditation, loosens tight muscles, relaxes your mind, and relieves general tension.

1 } Sit in a comfortable position and close your eyes. Keep your back straight, your shoulders down. Inhale slowly and deeply as you gently turn your head to the left, stretching your neck just to the point where you feel your muscles begin to resist.

2 } Exhale slowly as you gently turn your head to the right, stretching your neck just to the point where you feel your muscles begin to resist.

3 } Repeat. This time, stretch your neck a little further, but don't go beyond your point of comfort. Ease all thoughts from your mind.

4 } Pay attention to your movements and your breathing. Move slowly and deliberately—don't hurry or jerk—stretching your muscles only as far as feels comfortable.

5 } Inhale slowly and deeply, filling your stomach with air first, then your chest. Exhale slowly, releasing air from your chest first, then your stomach.

6 } Continue gently turning your head from one side to the other, inhaling as you turn to the left and exhaling as you turn to the right. Keep your mind calm and still. If thoughts arise into your awareness, choose to bring your attention back to your movements and breath.

7 } Continue doing this for as long as you like. When you feel looser and more relaxed, open your eyes.

Do this meditation for at least five minutes at a time, several times a day, to reduce computer-related stress.

WASH AWAY EVERYDAY IRRITATIONS

According to a theory proposed by Daniel Goleman, author of *The Meditative Mind*, and Tara Bennett-Goleman, author of *Emotional Alchemy: How the Mind Can Heal the Heart*, meditation affects the relationship between the amygdala and the prefrontal cortex in the brain. The amygdala governs fear responses and is linked with aggression; the prefrontal cortex causes you to pause, stay calm, and think before taking action. Meditation increases activity in the left prefrontal cortex so it prevails over the amygdala, thereby reducing tension, anxiety, and irritability.

The following meditation lets you wash away everyday annoyances and stress whenever you wash your body. Perform this simple practice in the morning, at night, or any time you wish to cleanse yourself of irritations.

1 } Stand in the bathroom shower and let the hot water pour down on you. Bring to mind a situation or an issue that is upsetting you. Think of that annoyance as dirt clinging to your body.

2 } As the hot water flows down your body, envision it washing away your concerns, anger, and anxiety. As you soap yourself, imagine you are cleansing stress from your body at the same time.

3 } Feel your muscles relaxing, your body growing lighter and freer as the shower massages your shoulders, back, and so on.

4 } As you shampoo, imagine you are also washing all your cares and aggravations out of your hair. Feel your mind clearing and growing calmer as you rinse the shampoo from your hair.

5 } Visualize all the irritations flowing down the drain, like dirty water.

6 } Continue to stand under the soothing shower spray for as long as you like, until you feel you are free of anger, anxiety, and irritability.

7 } When you're ready, step out of the shower, feeling relaxed and refreshed.

When it's not feasible to take a physical shower—when you're at the office or on a crowded subway, for example—you can do a variation of this meditation in your mind. Simply close your eyes and imagine you are standing in the shower or perhaps under a waterfall, letting the water wash your cares away.

FEEL REJUVENATED WITHIN YOUR SAFE HARBOR

What's your favorite element—air, fire, water, or earth? When you are in the presence of this element do you feel more at peace, more connected to your Soul and Spirit? Perhaps you feel more alive near a lake, a river, or the ocean. Or maybe walking in the woods is an enchanting experience for you. Do you feel a sense of liberation when standing high on a hill with the wind at your face? Or a special connection with a burning fire?

Whenever life's pressures build or the storms of responsibilities crash about you, you can always find a safe harbor within your particular element. The following meditation will help you.

~~~~~~~

1 } Sit or lie comfortably, with your eyes closed. Take a deep breath and exhale. Do this two more times. Relax using whichever method you prefer, such as focusing on your breath, envisioning a peaceful scene, or mentally relaxing each part of your body starting with your toes and working your way up to the top of your head. After you are relaxed, mentally count down from seven to one, relaxing more deeply with each count.

2 } On the count of one, find yourself in your Safe Place. Feel the beauty, love, blessed solitude, or enchantment of this place. Which of the four elements seems most present here—air, water, earth, or fire? Invite your Higher Self to join you. Sit together. Ask your Higher Self to take you to the "Place of Your Element."

3 } With your Higher Self, journey beyond your Safe Place. Travel over the changing terrain. Experience each of the elements along the way.

4 } In time you will come to a wondrous and magical place. It may be on a mountaintop or by a beach or lake. It may be on an open plain, in a sacred grotto, or in a warm, sunny place.

5 } Sit together in this place. Feel your element strongly here. Perhaps you didn't think this was your element. That's okay—it is. Experience the power, the majesty of this element. Let it elevate you. Feel your Soul nurturing you here, and your Spirit coming alive.

6 } Lie down in this magical place. Close your mental eyes and sense all the stress being drawn from you. Feel every part of your body being "refitted" and made whole. Feel yourself being loved and nurtured here. Feel at peace. Feel safe and protected. Feel alive. Feel at home.

(continued on page 34)

7 } Take as much time as you need to become charged, aligned, nurtured, and at one with yourself. When you are ready, close your mental eyes and count mentally from one to five. On the count of five, open your physical eyes and return.

Do this meditation any time you feel pressured, overwhelmed, or in need of love and nurturing. We also suggest finding a place near your home where your element is strongest. Go there on a regular basis. Lie down or sit comfortably in this place and, as you do in the meditation, let yourself be loved, recharged, and nurtured. Don't wait until you're stressed out to seek relief. Whether in meditation or in the outer world, you can always have a safe harbor to lay anchor when the seas of life become too turbulent.

WHAT'S YOUR ELEMENT?

To discover your element, don't think about your zodiac sign. Instead, consider your reactions to nature using these examples. Which of the following rings true for you? Each of us gravitates to one more than the others. You may love the ocean (water) and gardening (earth) but may have a deep "soulful" connection to fire (which, incidentally, is present in water and earth).

Earth

You feel a transcendent pleasure working in a garden. Walking in the woods or a forest is an enchanting experience for you. You feel a special kinship with trees, flowers, and other plants, and may have a green thumb.

Fire

You love sitting around a campfire or in front of a roaring fire in your fireplace. Lying on the beach beneath the hot sun nurtures you. Candlelight evokes a sense of magic and mystery for you. You feel awed by flashes of lightning.

Air

You feel a sense of liberation when standing high on a hill or a mountaintop. You love to feel the wind on your face. You enjoy being in wide-open spaces. Storms excite and invigorate you.

Water

You feel more alive when you're by or on a lake, a river, or the ocean. Walking in the rain is something magical and wonderful for you. Taking a bath or shower nurtures you.

TURN DOWN THE ANNOYANCE LEVEL IN YOUR ENVIRONMENT

According to the American Institute of Stress, workplace stress costs the United States $300 billion annually in medical care and employee absenteeism. A three-month study, published in 1993 in the journal *Anxiety, Stress, & Coping*, examined workers in the automotive industry to determine the effects of meditation on stress reduction. The study found that employees who meditated regularly experienced decreases in job tension, anxiety, fatigue, and health complaints.

It's not always easy to change conditions in your work environment. However, this meditation technique helps you deal with annoying people, workplace noise, and other stress by turning down the volume.

~~~~~~

1 } Isolate a particular noise that you find annoying. It might be someone's loud voice, the roar of a machine, traffic noise, or some other bothersome sound. Focus on that noise for a moment, trying to distinguish it from other sounds in your environment.

2 } Close your eyes and take a few slow, deep breaths. Bring to mind an image of a large, round dial, like the ones that used to be on TVs and radios. This dial controls the volume of the noise that you find annoying. Make the dial a bright color, such as red or orange.

3 } Now, imagine yourself reaching to grasp that dial. See and feel your fingers touch the dial. Take hold of the dial and begin slowly turning it to lower the volume.

4 } As you adjust the dial, notice the color starts to fade and become softer. See the dial begin to change color. Watch it gradually shift to a peaceful pale blue. As you turn the dial, you ratchet down the volume of the annoying noise.

5 } Continue turning the dial, lowering the noise level a little at a time. Feel yourself growing calmer and more relaxed.

6 } Sense yourself detaching from the annoying noise, until the sound no longer seems as bothersome.

7 } Keep turning down the volume until the noise becomes tolerable or even diminishes entirely from your awareness.

Perform this meditation whenever outside irritations threaten to upset your serenity. Rather than feeling like a victim, you take control of the situation. You can also use this practice at home, in the mall, at school—any place at all—to reduce annoyances in your environment.

RELEASE STRESS AT THE END OF THE DAY

Daytime stress often causes sleep dysfunction. You lie awake in bed, rehashing the events of the day and worrying about tomorrow's challenges, too keyed up to relax. When you don't get a good night's sleep, you're also likely to be more anxious and stressed out during the day. It's a vicious circle.

A study presented at the twenty-third Annual Meeting of the Associated Professional Sleep Societies in June 2009, and published in *ScienceDaily*, showed that meditation is effective in treating sleep problems. According to Ramadevi Gourineni, MD, director of the insomnia program at Northwestern Memorial Hospital in Evanston, Illinois, insomnia results from being in a state of hyperarousal around the clock. The following meditation helps you unwind at bedtime, so you enjoy more restful sleep. It also reduces stress during the day.

~~~~~~

1 } At night, lie in bed on your back or in a position that's comfortable for you. Close your eyes and begin breathing slowly, deeply. Turn your attention to your breathing.

2 } As you inhale, focus on your heart chakra, the energy center located in the chest region near your heart. Imagine you are taking into this chakra pure, clean, healing air. See or sense it filling your chest and circulating through your body.

3 } As you exhale, imagine releasing all the dirty, dark, stagnant air you've stored up during the day. See or sense this polluted air emptying from your body and flowing out through the soles of your feet and the palms of your hands.

4 } As the old air leaves your body, so does the stress you've accumulated during the day.

Imagine the irritations, upsets, and tension flowing out through the soles of your feet and the palms of your hands, leaving you feeling calm and relaxed.

5 } Continue breathing in this manner, keeping your attention focused on your breath. With each exhalation, your body and mind grow lighter and cleaner. With each inhalation, your body and mind become calmer and more relaxed.

6 } If your mind starts to wander or unwanted thoughts begin to intrude, gently let them go and turn your attention back to your breathing.

7 } Continue this pattern of air exchange, purifying your body of stress and impurities, until you fall asleep.

Perform this meditation each night as soon as you go to bed, to unwind and sleep better.

WALK A LABYRINTH TO FIND INNER PEACE

For thousands of years, people around the world have walked labyrinths for relaxation and spiritual purposes. As you meander through a labyrinth's circuitous form, you shift your awareness back and forth from right brain to left brain, creating harmony. One of the oldest labyrinth designs features seven "circuits" that correspond to the seven tones of the musical scale, the seven colors of the visible spectrum, the seven main chakras in the body, and the seven bodies in our solar system that can be seen with the naked eye. These relationships may explain why winding your way through a labyrinth balances the body's energy fields and inspires inner peace.

1 } Enter the labyrinth. Walk slowly and mindfully, paying attention to each step. Notice how the ground feels beneath your feet, how your body shifts as you walk.

2 } Let go of everyday concerns and thoughts about the world outside you. Don't worry about where you are in the labyrinth or where you're going. Unlike a maze, which has many blind alleys and dead ends, a labyrinth has only one twisting path that leads to the center and back out again.

3 } Allow your thoughts to turn inward. Moving to the center of the labyrinth symbolizes moving to the center of your own being. Continue purposefully placing one foot in front of the other until you reach the center of the labyrinth. Pause for as long as you like to enjoy feeling peaceful, centered, and calm. Experience your connection to the earth and sky.

4 } Close your eyes, if you like, and look deep into yourself. Notice any insights or feelings that arise. If you wish, mentally place an intention (for instance, to heal yourself or to attract prosperity) in the center of the labyrinth. The labyrinth's womblike shape nurtures your intention and helps it materialize.

5 } When you are ready, turn and begin retracing your steps, walking back out of the labyrinth. Walk slowly and mindfully, paying attention to each step. As you walk, gradually shift your awareness from your inner world to the outer one.

6 } When you reach the opening where you entered the labyrinth, pause for a moment to embrace the world outside and acknowledge your connection with all that is.

7 } Exit the labyrinth with a sense of gratitude and serenity.

Interestingly, you don't have to walk a labyrinth to experience its calming benefits. You can simply use the design shown here—run your finger through the circuits and see what happens.

RELEASE TENSION FROM TOE TO HEAD

Herbert Benson, MD, associate professor at Harvard Medical School and director emeritus of Harvard Medical School's Mind/Body Medical Institute and the Benson-Henry Institute, recommends consciously relaxing all your muscles one at a time while you meditate. He calls this the "relaxation response." Benson's research shows that meditation has a beneficial effect on metabolism, heart rate, respiration, blood pressure, and other biochemical and physical processes in the body.

The following meditation expands upon Dr. Benson's ideas, enabling you to relax and let go of tension in every part of your body. Like water flowing through a series of locks in a canal, energy flows up from your toes to your head as you do this meditation. We recommend taking your shoes off and wearing loose-fitting clothing to facilitate relaxation.

~~~~~~

1 } Lie on your back on the bed or in another place where you feel safe and comfortable. Lay your arms at your sides, palms facing up. Close your eyes and begin breathing slowly, deeply. When you feel somewhat relaxed, turn your attention to your toes.

2 } Curl your toes for a few moments, tightening the muscles in them, and then relax your toes. Feel comforting energy flow into your toes as you release the tension in them. By accentuating the tightness in your muscles, and then relaxing them, you are able to identify and more fully release the tension you've been holding there. Next, tense the muscles in your feet for a few moments, and then release them. Feel comforting energy flow into your relaxed feet. Tighten the muscles in your calves for a few moments, and then release them. Notice how energy surges up into your calves after you relax them. Tighten the muscles in your thighs for a few moments, and then release them. These powerful muscles are involved with support and movement, in both a physical and a symbolic sense.

3 } Tighten the muscles in your buttocks for a few moments, and then release them. You are now beginning to move energy upward from your tailbone along your spine, through the chakras. Notice any emotions that surface as you tense and relax these muscles. Shift your attention to your abdomen as you tighten the muscles there for a few moments. Release your muscles and let the energy flow into your abdomen. Now, tighten the muscles in your lower back for a few moments, and then release them. Feel soothing energy begin to flow up your spine, enlivening your chakras as well as your muscles. Tighten the muscles in your mid-back for a few moments, and then release them. Tighten the muscles in your chest for a few moments, and then release them. Feel loving vibrations spread out through

(continued on page 40)

your chest, stimulating your heart and heart chakra region. Tighten the muscles in your upper back for a few moments, and then release them. Notice how much tension you've been holding there. Feel yourself becoming more flexible and comfortable.

4} Tighten the muscles in your shoulders for a few moments, and then release them. Mentally shrug as you feel yourself shucking off the weight of the world that you've been shouldering. Tighten the muscles in your arms for a few moments, and then release them. Let go and let your arms hang loose as you feel energy flowing through them. Tighten the muscles in your hands and fingers for a few moments, and then release them. Feel energy resonating all the way out to your fingertips.

5} Tighten the muscles in your neck for a few moments, and then release them. Continue drawing life energy up your spine, allowing that energy to enliven every part of your body as it rises. Tighten the muscles in your face for a few moments. As you release your facial muscles, relax your jaw and feel rejuvenating energy spreading across your cheeks, chin, and brow. Tighten the muscles of your scalp for a few moments, and then release them. Allow energy to flow up and out through the crown of your head, connecting you with the healing force of the universe.

6} Your entire body now feels relaxed, balanced, and energized. All the tension your muscles once held has now been released. Spend as long as you like enjoying this calm, relaxed state of being.

7} When you're ready, open your eyes and gradually ease into your everyday routine.

Do this meditation whenever you feel a need to unwind and drop the cares of your everyday life. We suggest doing it at the end of a stressful day, to unwind before bedtime, or to leave behind your workday pressures and relax into your personal life.

A SCENT-SATIONAL WAY TO RELAX

Ayurvedic medicine considers bathing to be therapeutic. The healing benefits of bathing have been touted since ancient times—the Greeks and Romans believed water was a gift from the gods, and to that end, they created elaborate bathhouses for healing purposes.

Today, hydrotherapy continues to be prized as a healing modality. Bathing eases stiff muscles, relieves pain, opens clogged pores, stimulates circulation, and restores moisture to the body's tissues. In 1994, French researchers published a study in the *Journal of Rheumatology* that found that patients who underwent hydrotherapy "showed significant improvement" from lower back pain and other ailments. A few years later, a majority of test subjects in a University of Minnesota study confirmed these findings; furthermore, they agreed that therapeutic baths reduced their stress and anxiety levels.

This meditation combines the benefits of hydrotherapy, meditation, and aromatherapy to alleviate stress and enhance relaxation.

〜〜〜〜

1 } At the end of the day, draw a hot bath. Eliminate all distractions: phone calls, work and family demands, and so on.

2 } Add a few drops of lavender essential oil to the water. (Only pure essential oils contain aromatherapy properties—synthetic scents don't.) Turn off the lights and burn candles, if you wish. You may also choose to include relaxing music in your environment.

3 } Get into the bathtub, lean back, and relax. Allow the hot water to embrace you, easing your physical and mental tension. Feel the worries of the day slipping away. Put your attention on the sensations you feel.

4 } Keep your attention focused in the present and your enjoyment of it—set everyday cares and concerns aside for the moment. If unwanted thoughts arise, acknowledge and release them without judgment, then bring your attention back to the calming experience of bathing.

5 } Allow the fragrant scent of the lavender essential oil to calm your mind and help you release everyday worries and anxiety. For this brief time, allow yourself to feel totally relaxed, carefree, and pampered.

6 } Spend about fifteen to twenty minutes soaking in the bathtub. When you're ready, emerge from the tub feeling clean, relaxed, and rejuvenated.

7 } As the bathwater flows down the drain, imagine your cares and stress disappearing along with it.

Perform this meditation as often as you like—every evening, if possible—to release stress and anxiety at the end of the day.

EASE PREOPERATIVE STRESS

A pilot study, published in *Integrative Cancer Therapies* in 2008, examined meditation's ability to ease stress in patients undergoing hematopoietic stem cell transplants (HSCT) for various conditions, including cancer. Researchers found that patients who began meditation prior to surgery and continued through their recovery experienced "statistically significant decreases in heart and respiratory rates and improvements in symptoms" associated with stress.

Why do some people have less difficulty during medical procedures and recover more quickly than others? Much of it may be linked to their expectations and attitudes. Just because someone else has a hard time with a particular operation doesn't mean you will. Before you undergo a medical or dental procedure, utilize the following steps and the meditation given here to reduce emotional and physical stress.

~~~~~~

BEFORE THE OPERATION

1 } Imagine yourself within a cocoon of white protective light.

2 } Be aware that you are not alone—your Higher Self, Soul and Spirit, God and Goddess, Angels, and/or other deities are supporting you. Allow yourself to sense their loving presence as best you can.

3 } Know that the Higher Selves of the doctors, nurses, and medical staff will be present as well.

4 } Choose for this experience to be as effortless as possible, and know that you will grow and learn as a result of it, and emerge healthier and happier.

THE MEDITATION

1 } Sit or lie comfortably, with your eyes closed. Take a deep breath and exhale. Do this two more times. Relax using whichever method you prefer. After you are relaxed, mentally count down from seven to one, relaxing more deeply with each count.

2 } On the count of one, find yourself in your Safe Place. Feel the beauty, love, blessed solitude, or enchantment of this place. Invite your Higher Self to join you. Tell your Higher Self that you choose for this operation to be one of ease, healing on all levels, and growth.

3 } Now, search within yourself to see if you may be harboring any resentment, anger, self-pity, or other feelings that might interfere with your conscious intentions. (See "You Always Get What You Want [Although It May Not Be What You Ask For]" on page 18.) Invite these feelings to present themselves so you can address them. See them personified as a figure we'll call your Martyr.

4 } Ask your Martyr to speak. It may be angry or fearful. It might vent in a number of ways. Listen to it, without interrupting. When your Martyr is done, tell it, "You may not participate in this operation or my recovery." Be firm, and it will then fade away.

5 } Now, lie back in your Higher Self's arms and close your mental eyes. Imagine you are safe within a cocoon of white light. Imagine undergoing all phases of the operation or procedure from pre-op, to the operation or procedure itself, to the post-op recovery. See or sense the presence of the Higher Selves of everyone who is involved. You might see them as beings of light, or something else. You are not alone and you are loved, protected, and cared for. Sense the whole experience transpiring smoothly, without discomfort of any kind.

6 } Now, imagine yourself at home and completely recovered. Feel joy, exhilaration, freedom, and peace of mind after having undergone a most amazing and effortless experience. When you are done, open your mental eyes. You are still safe in your Higher Self's arms. Sit up and notice, beyond the bounds of your Safe Place, the Future You who is completely recovered in a most elegant way. Invite this Future You to enter your Safe Place. Stand facing each other. Gaze deeply into each other's eyes. Begin breathing together, in sync. Inhale, exhale. Inhale, exhale. Then, all of a sudden, both of you take a deep breath and as you exhale, your present and future selves become one.

7 } Thank your Higher Self. Close your mental eyes and mentally count from one to five. On the count of five, open your physical eyes and return.

Do this meditation every day for at least two weeks prior to the operation or procedure. If you are in an emergency situation, at least follow the "Before the Operation" steps.

USE A CRYSTAL TO RELIEVE STRESS AND TENSION

Computers utilize quartz's unique ability to gather, hold, and transmit information. But long before computers existed, quartz crystals were prized for their healing abilities. The same properties that enable crystals to handle information in computers make them effective in balancing and aligning energy within your body. Just as you can program a computer to do whatever you want it to, so too can you program a crystal to assist you in myriad ways. This meditation helps you work with a quartz crystal to relieve daily stress and tension.

~~~~~

BEFORE YOU BEGIN

1 } Acquire a quartz crystal with which to work. We recommend choosing a quartz crystal sphere no smaller than 3 inches (5 cm) in diameter. If a sphere is not available, any quartz "generator" (a common type of crystal) no less than 3 inches (5 cm) in length will work just fine. You can purchase crystals at New Age stores, at gem and mineral shops, and from many online sites.

2 } After you acquire your crystal, hold it under running tepid water for a few moments to clean it. Next, rub your thumb quickly across its side, blowing sharply over the crystal as you rub. Rub and blow simultaneously. This will release any programs the crystal's previous keepers may have put there, as well as any "gunk" that may have collected within it.

3 } Now, mentally instruct the crystal to draw out all stress from your system. Hold this intent in your mind as you blow it into the crystal with a quick, short breath. The crystal is now ready to do its work.

THE MEDITATION

1 } Lie down on your bed or sit in a comfortable place and close your eyes. Take a deep breath and exhale. Do this two more times. Allow yourself to relax for a moment or two.

2 } Holding the quartz crystal in both hands, place it on your stomach.

3 } See or sense all your stress leaving you and moving into the crystal. If you can visualize the stress leaving, great. If not, just feel it leaving you. Feel the crystal drawing out the stress as well. Spend at least three minutes doing this.

4 } Now, with both hands holding the crystal, place it on your heart. Again, mentally send all your stress into the crystal. See or feel it leaving you. Feel the crystal drawing out the stress as well. Do this for at least three minutes.

5 } Finally, with both hands, hold the crystal to your forehead. Mentally send all your stress and tension into the crystal. If you have a headache, see or feel the headache leaving you. Feel the crystal drawing out the stress and pain as well. Do this for at least three minutes.

6 } When you feel relaxed and serene, open your eyes.

7 } Thank the crystal for its assistance.

After every meditation, cleanse your crystal by holding it under running tepid water. When done, rub your thumb sharply across its side while simultaneously blowing sharply over the crystal to release the stress and tension placed within. If you don't clear and release your crystal, you run the risk of replacing the stress back into you the next time you use the crystal. You could also damage your crystal.

NAVIGATE THROUGH A CRISIS

As the ancient Greek philosopher Heraclitus put forth 2,500 years ago, change is central to the universe. Like everything in creation, we are changing, growing, and evolving. Even positive change—a new job, a wedding, the birth of a baby—can cause stress. When change comes so fast that we don't have time to deal with it or integrate it, we invariably find ourselves in a crisis. A crisis is not a fun place to be, but we can minimize its intensity and duration by choosing to navigate through it rather than resisting or giving in to it.

In a study published in *Medical News Today* in 2008, researchers at the Benson-Henry Institute at Massachusetts General Hospital examined subjects to see how meditation influenced their stress response. The researchers found that meditation produced physiological reactions that were the opposite of the reactions induced by posttraumatic stress disorder.

The following meditation can be a wonderful companion before and/or during periods of stress and crisis.

~~~~~~

1 } Sit or lie comfortably, with your eyes closed. Take a deep breath and exhale. Do this two more times. Relax using whichever method you prefer. After you are somewhat relaxed, mentally count down from seven to one, relaxing more deeply with each count.

2 } On the count of one, find yourself in your Safe Place. Feel the beauty, love, blessed solitude, or enchantment of this place. Invite your Higher Self to join you. Sit together. Talk of your crisis. When you are done, close your mental eyes and count from five to one.

3 } On the count of one, open your mental eyes and find yourself at the helm of a sailboat. Your Higher Self is beside you at the helm. The water is still and the wind is light. The sky is hazy. It is neither a good day nor a bad day—a dull, uneventful day. Your boat is moving very slowly, and you feel a little listless and indifferent. After a while, you notice in the distance the sky is dark and foreboding. A major storm is approaching. You are now faced with three choices: turn back, stop and wait it out, or sail into it.

4 } You decide to point the bow of your boat directly into the storm and sail forward. The sea gets rougher and the wind picks up, but your Higher Self is behind you with both hands on the wheel next to yours. You enter the storm. The winds howl, and the sea crashes about your boat. Lightning flashes; thunder roars and the wind bellows. But you keep your boat steady, heading forward and on course. Feel the intensity of the storm. Everything around you is wild and chaotic, but you are safe and on course.

5 } Now you feel the wind behind you, filling your sails and blowing you forward. The lightning illuminates the way ahead. It seems as if the gale is more an ally than an antagonist. Keep your boat heading forward, on course.

6 } Eventually you notice the dark clouds breaking up and beams of sunlight shining through. The winds diminish; the thunder and lightning fade into the distance behind you. The water is calm and a steady breeze blows at your back. You steer your boat in newer waters now, moving smoothly and swiftly forward.

7 } You have made it through the gale. You have succeeded. Feel the triumph and exhilaration of your accomplishment. Feel excited and thrilled to be once again moving on course to your destiny. You are the captain of your ship and you have sailed her well. Celebrate and move forward. Thank your Higher Self, and close your mental eyes. Mentally count from one to five. On the count of five, open your physical eyes and return.

Crisis often occurs after your life has languished in the doldrums, when things seem neither good nor bad, just "blah." Do this meditation whenever you sense a crisis approaching. During the crisis, do this meditation each day to help you navigate more smoothly and quickly through it.

PART

3

You've heard the old saying "an apple a day keeps the doctor away," but the same can be said of meditation. Health insurance statistics showed that people who meditated regularly had significantly fewer inpatient and outpatient hospital visits than non-meditators—about half as many for young adults and approximately 70 percent fewer for adults over the age of forty, according to a report published in *Psychosomatic and Behavioral Medicine*. Hospital admissions were lower for meditators in categories ranging from malignant tumors to heart disease.

MEDITATIONS FOR
PHYSICAL
HEALING

BOLSTER YOUR IMMUNE SYSTEM

Meditation may offer a cure for the common cold and flu. An eight-week clinical study, headed by Richard J. Davidson, PhD, of the Laboratory for Affective Neuroscience, University of Wisconsin, and published in the journal *Psychosomatic Medicine* in 2003, found that meditation can enhance the body's immune function. The research showed that meditation activated the left-side anterior regions of the brain (associated with positive emotions and relaxation) and significantly increased the amount of antibodies (which protect the body against foreign substances) in the blood of subjects who meditated.

The following meditation uses visualization to marshal your body's natural defenses to combat infections of all kinds. Practice this technique to strengthen your immune system so you recover more quickly from colds, flu, and other ailments.

~~~~~~

1 } In a place where you feel comfortable and safe, sit or lie quietly with your eyes closed. Take a deep breath and exhale. Do this two more times. Relax using whichever method you prefer. Count down mentally from seven to one, relaxing further with each count.

2 } On the count of one, turn your attention to the area of your body where the illness or other problem exists. Observe the cells in this part of your body. Notice that some of the cells appear damaged or irregular in some way. You may see them as misshapen, inflamed, or of an ugly, dull color. These are the unhealthy cells associated with your illness.

3 } As you continue to observe your body, you'll also notice many cells that look strong and vital. These cells are well formed and whole. They may be a bright, beautiful color or seem to glow with a radiant white light. These are your healthy cells. The healthy cells are part of your body's natural defense system. They protect you against harmful cells that invade and impair your body.

4 } Imagine the healthy cells surrounding and permeating the unhealthy ones. Sense the healthy cells absorbing and transforming the unhealthy ones into brilliant healthy cells. Observe the action until all the cells have been transformed into luminescent, healthy cells.

5 } Your body is now completely free of illness and radiant with health. Watch as the healthy cells repair any damage left behind by the unhealthy cells. Notice that the area where the illness once existed is now glowing with radiant white light.

6 } Visualize and feel your body completely healthy, strong, and whole. Hold this image in your mind for as long as you wish. Feel what you would feel being healthy and free of the malady.

7 } When you feel ready, close your mental eyes and count mentally from one to five. On the count of five, open your physical eyes.

Spend at least ten minutes performing this meditation twice a day—first thing in the morning and last thing at night—during an illness. You can do it more often throughout the day, if you like, to speed recovery.

BREATHE DEEPLY TO LOWER YOUR BLOOD PRESSURE

According to the American Heart Association, more than 73 million people in the United States over the age of twenty—one in three adults—have high blood pressure. In 2005, high blood pressure was the primary or a contributing cause in the deaths of 319,000 Americans. The American Heart Association's journal *Hypertension* reported in November 1995 and August 1996 that meditation can be as effective as antihypertensive drugs in reducing blood pressure in both men and women—without the unwanted side effects.

~~~~~~

1 } Lie on your back in a quiet place where you feel safe and comfortable. Put a pillow under your knees to elevate them slightly, so they are several inches higher than your heart and your head. Place your right palm on your abdomen, and lay your left arm along your side, palm facing up.

2 } Close your eyes and begin breathing slowly and deeply. Turn your attention to your breathing. As you inhale, count slowly to six. Fill your stomach with air first. Feel your stomach rise as it expands to take in oxygen-rich air. Continue inhaling slowly, filling your lungs with air. Notice how your chest opens and rises as you breathe in.

3 } When you feel full, hold your breath for a count of four. Exhale slowly, to a count of six. Release the air from your lungs and chest first, then your stomach. Pull your stomach in toward your backbone, emptying yourself completely of air.

4 } Repeat, keeping your attention focused on your breathing. With each inhalation, you take in refreshing, rejuvenating oxygen that nourishes every cell in your body. With each exhalation, you release tension and impurities from your body.

5 } If distracting thoughts come into your mind, simply let them go without judgment, and return your attention to your breathing.

6 } Feel yourself simultaneously becoming more relaxed, centered, and revitalized.

7 } Continue breathing in this manner for at least ten minutes.

Perform this meditation twice daily, once in the morning and once in the evening, to reduce tension and keep your blood pressure in the normal range. If at any time you begin to sense your blood pressure rising due to stress, shift your attention to your breathing.

AN ENJOYABLE WAY TO STOP SMOKING

An analysis of 198 independent outcomes, published in *Alcoholism Treatment Quarterly* in 1994, found that meditation provided greater reductions in tobacco, alcohol, and nonprescription drug use than the usual substance abuse treatments. Additionally, the improvements derived from meditation continued to increase over time.

Arizona State University's Michael Winkelman, PhD, MPH, explains meditation's success this way: "Psychobiological perspectives . . . on natural ASC [altered states of consciousness] indicate they are both useful as a prophylactic against drug abuse, as well as a potential treatment for addiction. These ASC can provide an alternative source of transcendence to the drugs of addiction, facilitating a smoother transition to the path of recovery."

Most people are unaware of their smoking most of the time. Instead of a form of pleasure, smoking becomes an unpleasant habit, a poor substitute for nurturing. The following meditation suggests that if you focus totally on enjoying the cigarette, your cigarette use will drastically decrease. Using this method, people often cut down from two or three packs a day to, perhaps, two or three cigarettes a day—and do so pleasurably. The meditation has three essential rules:

～～～～

1 } Catch yourself when you reach for a cigarette.
2 } Stop all other activity while smoking.
3 } Totally enjoy smoking the cigarette.

No matter what you are engaged in, when you notice yourself reaching for a cigarette, stop whatever you're doing and focus totally on smoking the cigarette. If you're driving, pull over and smoke the cigarette. If you are in the company of other people, excuse yourself and go someplace private to smoke. Under no circumstances should you do anything other than enjoy the cigarette. Give your complete attention to the pleasure of smoking. When you've finished, return to what you were doing.

(continued on page 54)

It will seem awkward at first, but discipline yourself to stick to all three rules. Your success depends on this. The tricky part initially is catching yourself as you reach for the cigarette. Don't be hard on yourself if you only manage to catch yourself occasionally in the beginning. Keep at it—it will get progressively easier.

The act of enjoying the cigarette is the meditation itself. The key is *enjoyment*. Set an intention to be totally aware when you are smoking. Settle down into the process. Feel the pleasurable sensations associated with smoking. Feel nurtured by it. Let the smoking be a wondrous time of musing—no struggle, no pressure, no guilt, and no effort. Be gentle with yourself.

In time, you'll discover you need fewer cigarettes to satisfy your cravings—and when you do smoke you'll enjoy it more. You might even stop smoking altogether.

APPLY LOVING HANDS TO EASE PAIN

Fifty million people worldwide suffer from chronic pain. In a study done at the University of California, Irvine, and published in *NeuroReport* in 2006, researchers found that longtime meditators showed a 40 to 50 percent lower brain response to pain than people who didn't meditate. When the study's control group learned meditation and practiced it for five months, their reaction to pain also dropped by 40 to 50 percent.

The purpose of pain is to warn you that something needs attention—yes, something physical, but in a more real sense, something emotional. Easing pain is important, but *healing* pain requires paying attention to deeper feelings. One way to work with pain is to personify it. Talk to the personified pain. Listen to it without judgment or self-blame. Most important, feel the emotions beneath the physical pain. When you're ready, forgive yourself, and ask that the pain be released. The following meditation can ease discomfort while you're healing.

~~~~~

1 } Sit or lie comfortably, with your eyes closed. Take a deep breath and exhale. Do this two more times. Relax using whichever method you prefer. After you are somewhat relaxed, mentally count down from seven to one, relaxing more deeply with each count.

2 } On the count of one, find yourself in your Safe Place at evening time (evening time in the meditation). Use your inner sense(s) to make this place more real to you.

3 } Notice your Higher Self standing by a "healing bed." It might be a soft bed of flowers, silk or satin, or perhaps downy feathers. It may be illuminated by candlelight and surrounded by crystals. Let what appears, appear. Sense this healing place as comfortable, beautiful, enchanting, magical, and loving.

4 } Approach your Higher Self. Stand facing each other. Feel your Higher Self's love for you. Let your Higher Self lovingly and gently remove your clothes and lower you onto the bed.

5 } Close your mental eyes and feel the stillness. Feel the magic, the love, the enchantment. Your Higher Self gently places its hand(s) upon your pain, sending a soothing warm light to you.

6 } See or sense the light surrounding the area of pain, absorbing or transmuting it.

7 } When the pain diminishes or is gone, close your mental eyes and mentally count from one to five.

8 } Open your physical eyes on the count of five.

Do this meditation every day until the pain subsides. When you are satisfied that this meditation is helping you, try sending a flowing stream of light from your heart to your hands, and then to the affected area when you aren't meditating.

DIALOGUE WITH YOUR CANCER

"There is evidence to show that suppressed anger can be a precursor to the development of cancer, and also a factor in its progression after diagnosis," reported *Cancer Nursing* in October 2000. Meditation improves cancer patients' quality of life, according to a two-year trial of 130 breast cancer patients conducted at Saint Joseph Hospital in Chicago and published in the journal *Integrative Cancer Therapies* in 2009. The study's author, Sanford Nidich, senior researcher at the Institute for Natural Medicine and Prevention, explained, "Emotional and psychosocial stress contribute to the onset and progression of breast cancer and cancer mortality." Meditation, by reducing stress, may also help prevent cancer and increase life expectancy after diagnosis.

If you have cancer, your body isn't whispering that something needs your attention—it's shouting. Cancer holds very deep emotions, most specifically anger. These emotions are in serious need of release. This does not mean venting all the time. It means "touching" your anger, instead of just letting it "touch" you. Ask your Higher Self for help. The answer will always be "Yes." Use the following meditation, as well as "Unblock Your Creativity" in part 10, to help you process and release blockages.

~~~~~~

1 } Sit or lie comfortably, with your eyes closed. Take a deep breath and exhale. Do this two more times. Relax using whichever method you prefer. After you are somewhat relaxed, mentally count down from seven to one, relaxing more deeply with each count.

2 } On the count of one, find yourself in your Safe Place. Use your inner sense(s) to make this place more real to you. Invite your Higher Self to join you here. Sit with your Higher Self. Be together; love together. Talk of the cancer and your desire, not just to make it go away, but also to heal it and the issues connected with it.

3 } Ask your Higher Self to take you to the place where the cancer resides. Together you begin a journey, beyond the bounds of your Safe Place. Eventually you come to a dark, frightening place. Maybe it's a deep cave, a desolate landscape, a swamp, or a dark forest. This is the Abode of Your Cancer. Sitting with your Higher Self, call forth your cancer. Demand it join you, here.

4 } Let it appear to you, personified. It may look like a monster, a wild beast, or a dark whirl of energy. Remember, the unconscious speaks in myth, metaphor, archetype, or symbol. How the cancer appears to you is part of the message; pay attention to it.

5 } With courage and steadfastness, ask your personified cancer to tell you what it needs to heal. Ask it to vent, rage, or otherwise express itself to you. Let it act up, act out. Let it have voice. Do not debate, argue, or reason with it. Just listen and feel its anger, hurt, loneliness, despair, shame, pain, or fear. The deeper you feel, the deeper the healing will be.

6 } When the cancer has finished expressing, thank it, love it, forgive it, and ask for its release. The image will fade away.

7 } Now, close your mental eyes and mentally count from one to five. On the count of five, open your physical eyes and return.

Do this meditation often. Be real. Be present. Be vulnerable. Be helped.

DISSOLVE CANCER CELLS WITH LOVE'S LASER

Roughly 40 percent of the population will be diagnosed with cancer at some time in their lives. The American Cancer Society estimates there will be five million new cases in the United States annually. Stress reduction is one of meditation's significant benefits in the treatment of cancer. As Charles L. Raison, MD, clinical director of the Mind-Body Program at Emory University School of Medicine in Atlanta, points out, "We know stress is a contributor to all the major modern killers."

In response to stress, the adrenals increase production of the hormone cortisol. One study of women with early stage breast cancer, published in 2008 in *Brain Behavior and Immunology*, found that meditation reduced the patients' levels of cortisol, improved their immune function, and enhanced their overall quality of life. The following meditation is designed to trigger vital hormonal and chemical changes necessary in healing cancer.

~~~~~~

1 } Sit or lie comfortably, with your eyes closed. Take a deep breath and exhale. Do this two more times. Relax using whichever method is comfortable for you. After you are somewhat relaxed, mentally count down from seven to one, relaxing more deeply with each count.

2 } On the count of one, find yourself in your Safe Place at evening time (evening in the meditation). Use your inner sense(s) to make this place more real to you. You will find your Higher Self waiting there, standing by a "healing bed." This could be a soft bed of flowers, downy feathers, sheets of silk or satin, or whatever appears to you. The space may be illuminated by candlelight and surrounded by crystals. Let whatever appears, appear. This healing place is comfortable, beautiful, enchanting, magical, and loving.

3 } Approach your Higher Self. Stand facing each other. Feel your Higher Self's love for you. Let your Higher Self lovingly and gently remove your clothes and lower you upon the bed. Close your mental eyes and feel the stillness. Feel the magic, the love, the enchantment.

4 } Let your attention go to the part of your body that is affected by cancer. See the cancer cells as best you can. Now, imagine the area becoming illuminated. See or sense your Higher Self gently placing its hands over the affected area. Feel your Higher Self sending a laser beam of bright white light into the affected area.

5 } With your mental eyes still closed, visualize the laser beam piercing the cancer cells (not attacking them). Feel the warmth, or heat, of the laser beam. You may even hear a faint tonal sound. See or sense the laser beam dissolving each cell. The laser beam isn't killing the cells; it's absorbing them to transmute their energy later.

6 } Continue in this manner until you sense that the laser has absorbed all the cancer cells. When the cells are gone, or you feel it's time to end this session, close your mental eyes and mentally count from one to five.

7 } On the count of five, open your physical eyes and return.

Do this meditation every day for at least twenty minutes at a time, for a minimum of two weeks. After two weeks, do the meditation at least once per week.

CHANT TO PURIFY YOUR BODY AND MIND

Many meditations include chanting as a way of tuning and purifying the body and mind. You can chant alone or with others; you can even combine chanting with music, dancing, clapping, or drumming. The sounds, resonating through your body, produce profound relaxation and heightened awareness that can support any type of healing. Just as ultrasound breaks up physical blockages, chanting breaks up energetic blockages in the body. According to Jonathan Goldman, musician, sound healer, and author of *Healing Sounds*, "Sound amplifies the power of conscious prayer."

If you don't have a personal mantra, you can chant the sound *Om*.

~~~~~~

1 } Sit in a comfortable position and close your eyes.

2 } Take a deep breath. As you exhale, intone the sound *Om*.

3 } Draw out the syllable slowly so it sounds like three syllables: AAAUUUMMMMMMMMMMM.

4 } Allow the vibration to resonate throughout your body.

5 } Hold the note for as long as possible, until you run out of breath. Feel a sense of calm, balance, and serenity.

6 } Repeat.

7 } Continue for as long as you like, but do it at least three times.

Another chant you may wish to use is *om mani padme hum*. Known as the chant of purification, it affirms that within each of us is the kernel of purity that can transform our human limitations and imperfections, enabling us to achieve the enlightened state of Buddhahood.

Many chants involve God names or spiritual words. However, words that convey positive images can also produce beneficial effects. The experiments conducted by Japanese scientist Masaru Emoto (published in his books *Messages from Water* and *The Hidden Message in Water*) demonstrated that words spoken in the near proximity of water, thought or mentally envisioned into water, or written on paper and taped to a container holding water can alter the molecular structure of the water and cause it to form into distinct shapes. Words such as *love*, *joy*, and *peace* produced beautiful snowflakelike shapes, whereas words such as *hate* caused broken, distorted forms.

Choose a word that feels good to you, that engenders positive thoughts and emotions. Usually, mundane words such as *car*, *house*, or *book* won't produce the results you desire.

If you like, you can use beads as part of your chanting ritual. Fingering a *mala*, a string of 108 beads, while meditating and chanting by yourself is called *japa*. Hold each bead individually between your thumb and index finger while you utter a chant—in much the same way as a Catholic prays with a rosary. Touching the beads activates acupressure points in your fingertips to enhance the meditative process.

USE YOGA TO UNBLOCK YOUR HEART

According to the American Heart Association, coronary disease is the leading cause of death in America today. More than 17 million people in the United States suffer from heart disease. A sixteen-week clinical trial of 103 patients with heart disease, published in the American Medical Association's *Archives of Internal Medicine* in 2006, found that daily meditation can decrease risk factors associated with coronary disease. The following meditation uses a yoga technique to help open your heart and improve coronary function.

1 } In a place where you feel comfortable and safe, stand or sit quietly with your eyes closed.

2 } Lift your shoulders and head, keeping your back and neck straight. Gently pull your shoulders back, as if trying to make your shoulder blades touch each other.

3 } Lift your chest, and feel it opening. Begin breathing slowly and deeply into your chest. Continue pulling your shoulders back gently, increasing the stretch across your chest. Feel your heart opening as you breathe deeply, filling it with life-giving oxygen.

4 } Feel your heart beating calmly, steadily, and fully with each breath. Stay focused on your breathing. If thoughts intrude into your consciousness, just let them go without judgment and turn your attention back to your breathing.

5 } Continue letting your heart open to embrace love, joy, and life. Breathe in this manner, keeping your shoulders back, your back and neck straight, for five minutes, or as long as is comfortable for you.

6 } When you've finished, relax and open your eyes.

7 } Shrug your shoulders for a few moments; breathe naturally.

Practice this meditation twice each day, once in the morning and once in the evening, or more often if you like.

HEAL HIDDEN ISSUES WITH CHAKRA LIGHT

According to Ayurvedic medicine, the chakras are energy centers positioned roughly from the top of the head to the base of the spine. The chakras overlap the two chains of nerve bundles located on either side of the spinal cord. Invisible to most people, these three-dimensional vortices of light influence us physically, mentally, emotionally, and spiritually. These vortices, however, can affect regions other than those with which they're usually associated.

Sometimes, hidden issues cause imbalances that overlap and express in parts of the body that may seem unrelated. Let's say, for example, that you have a diagnosed heart condition. The heart is influenced by the fourth, or "heart," chakra. But, if you feel insecure and fearful about love, this "overlap energy" could be sending you a signal. The healing solution could be to shine the light of the first chakra (the security center) onto your heart.

Your unconscious knows the origins of all health problems, as well as what's needed for their resolution. Allow your unconscious to determine which chakra influence is needed to heal your condition. In this meditation, don't try to determine what's supposed to happen—just let it come.

~~~~~~

1 } Sit or lie comfortably, with your eyes closed. Take a deep breath and exhale. Do this two more times. Relax using whichever method is comfortable to you. After you are somewhat relaxed, mentally count down from seven to one, relaxing more deeply with each count.

2 } On the count of one, find yourself in your Safe Place. Use your inner sense(s) to make this place more real to you. Invite your Higher Self to join you in this place. Sit together. Be together. Love together. Speak to your Higher Self about your physical ailment. Describe what you know of it. Speak of the issues that you are aware of, and of your desire to bring to the surface any issues yet unknown.

3 } When you've finished, lie down in your Safe Place and close your mental eyes. Let your attention go to the site of your physical ailment. A sphere of light will appear. It will be the color of one of the seven chakras: red, orange, yellow, green, blue, indigo, or white. Do not judge or manipulate it.

4 } The sphere of light will surround and bathe the ailing part of your body in its healing light, flowing around and through this area. Feel it! Let whatever emotions emerge come to the surface. Even if they're unpleasant emotions (more likely than not, they will be), have the courage to feel them.

THE CHAKRAS

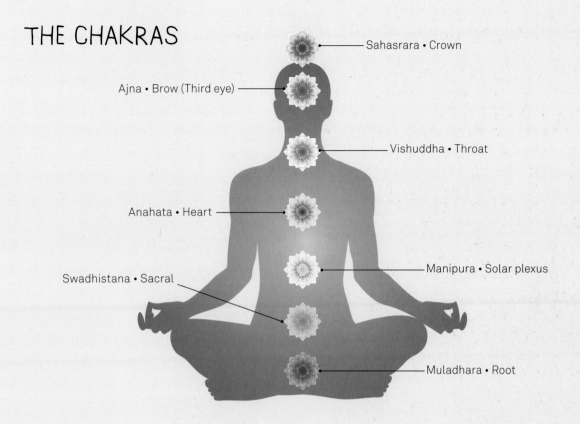

Sahasrara • Crown

Ajna • Brow (Third eye)

Vishuddha • Throat

Anahata • Heart

Manipura • Solar plexus

Swadhistana • Sacral

Muladhara • Root

5 } In time, the colored sphere of light will be completely absorbed in and around the body part or region. Open your mental eyes.

6 } Let your Higher Self hold you, love you, and heal you. Thank your Higher Self and close your mental eyes again.

7 } Count mentally from one to five. On the count of five, open your physical eyes and return.

Do this meditation every day for whatever period of time you sense is right. Don't be surprised if different colored spheres of light appear in different meditations.

Destructive emotions are any emotions—positive or negative—that you don't allow yourself to feel. Constructive emotions are any emotions—positive or negative—that you do allow yourself to feel, and in the case of the negative emotions, to release. Fully accessing all emotions is vital to emotional healing. In thirty years of working with clients using meditation as a chief component in the healing regimen, Martin has found that one of meditation's most powerful therapeutic benefits is freeing deep emotions and aiding their release.

MEDITATIONS FOR
EMOTIONAL
HEALING

BURN INCENSE TO CALM ANXIETY

According to a 1977 study published in the *Journal of Clinical Psychology*, meditation reduced anxiety. Twelve years later, in 1989, the journal looked at 146 independent meditation studies. The analysis reaffirmed meditation's effectiveness in lowering anxiety.

Incense burning began in Japan around 600 C.E. Often used as a meditation aid, incense means "to make sacred" in Latin. In Buddhist ceremonies, it is burned as an offering to invoke the Buddha's presence. Because inhaling aromatic substances affects the limbic system of the brain, the seat of emotions, burning the types of incense listed in this meditation can also help ease anxiety.

1 } Choose stick, cone, or coil incense that is made of pure plant materials and free of artificial ingredients. Choose incense in one or more of the following scents: sandalwood, lavender, vanilla, frankincense, clary sage, bergamot, or benzoin.

2 } Fit the incense in a fireproof burner, and light it. Blow out the flame and let the incense slowly smolder, emitting fragrant smoke into the air. Set the incense in a spot where it can continue to burn safely.

3 } Sit or lie in a place where you feel safe and comfortable, several feet away from the incense.

4 } Close your eyes and begin to relax using whichever method you prefer. Focus your attention on the aroma of the burning incense.

5 } As you inhale, feel the soothing scent calming your brain, silencing all thoughts and worries. As you exhale, feel the tension in your chest and abdomen relax as the anxiety leaves your body.

6 } Continue breathing in this manner for at least ten minutes, or as long as is comfortable for you, keeping your attention focused on inhaling and exhaling the pleasing aroma.

7 } When you feel ready, open your eyes.

Perform this meditation at least once a day, or any time you feel anxious.

MANAGE ANGER BY DISCONNECTING YOUR "BUTTONS"

As stress increases in our lives, so do anger and aggression. More than 25,000 murders are committed in the United States annually. In the workplace, five million people are assaulted each year, according to the Bureau of Labor Statistics. Add to those figures domestic violence, road rage, and other violent expressions of anger and it's apparent we need a strategy for anger management. The meditation below helps defuse anger by enabling you to detach from exterior stimuli.

Researchers from China and the University of Oregon studied college students to see how meditation affected their reactions to stress and their ability to resolve conflict. The findings, published in the *Proceedings of the National Academy of Sciences* in 2007, revealed that the students who meditated exhibited less stress, anxiety, and anger. Even people at the higher end of the anger-violence scale can benefit from meditation. A study of 1,350 inmates at six Massachusetts correctional facilities, published in *The Prison Journal* in 2007, found that meditation reduced hostility among both male and female prisoners.

~~~~~

1 } Sit or lie comfortably, with your eyes closed. Begin breathing slowly, deeply. Relax using whichever method you prefer.

2 } When you feel somewhat relaxed, imagine a line of red buttons running down the front of your body. Each of these buttons is connected to your anger center by a thin, sensitive wire. When someone "pushes your buttons" you experience a reaction.

3 } Call to mind a recent situation to which you responded with anger—perhaps an argument with a family member, a traffic jam, or a disagreement at work. See or sense someone reaching out and pushing one of your red buttons. Feel yourself instantly react with annoyance, anger, or hostility.

4 } Mentally take a pair of scissors and cut through the wire that attaches the button to your anger, deactivating it. Now, see or sense the person pressing that red button again. This time, nothing happens. You feel no reaction because the button has been disconnected. Realize that the other person has no ability to affect you once you've defused the button. Feel the sense of calm and relief that result from not reacting.

5 } Bring to mind another incident of anger. See or sense someone pushing another one of your red buttons. Feel yourself react with anger.

6 } Mentally snip the wire that connects this button to your anger. See or sense the person pushing this button again. Now, nothing happens. You don't feel anything or respond in any way. Repeat this procedure until you've deactivated all your buttons.

7 } When you've finished, spend a few minutes enjoying your newfound sense of tranquility and freedom. Realize that you don't need to react to other people or give them the power to manipulate your emotional responses. When you're ready, open your eyes.

Do this meditation regularly to diminish your tendency to react angrily to external stimuli. Any time you feel pressured to respond angrily to a person or situation, do this meditation to restore your equilibrium and keep your cool.

RELEASE UNWANTED HABITS AND BEHAVIORS

A three-month study of the effects of stress, published in the journal *Anxiety, Stress, & Coping* in 1993, found that along with reducing stress, meditation also helped alleviate other health and lifestyle problems. Subjects who meditated regularly decreased their use of cigarettes and hard liquor (beer and wine were not mentioned in the survey) and experienced less anxiety and fatigue. As a result, their general health improved and so did their personal and work relationships.

Self-limiting behaviors such as overeating, alcoholism, obsessive-compulsive behavior, smoking, drug use, television addiction, and so on are often linked with both stress and poor self-esteem. The following meditation helps you reprogram your thinking and release unwanted attitudes and behaviors by enabling you to see yourself in a new light.

~~~~~~~

1 } Sit or lie comfortably, with your eyes closed. Relax using whichever method you prefer. After you are somewhat relaxed, mentally count down from seven to one, relaxing more deeply with each number.

2 } On the count of one, sense that you are in your Safe Place. Use your inner sense(s) to make this place more real to you.

3 } When you feel ready, bring your attention to the point between your eyebrows that is sometimes called the "third eye." Also known as the *Asna*, or brow chakra, this energy center is associated with your perceptions. Through this chakra you receive information intuitively and see beyond the range of your physical sight.

4 } Call to mind the habit, attitude, or self-limiting behavior you wish to release, such as overly judgmental thinking or obsessive-compulsive actions. Acknowledge and experience any feelings of inadequacy, doubt, or self-criticism that may arise.

5 } Keep focusing on your brow chakra. Even though your eyes are closed, you may want to roll your eyes slightly so they look up and inward, toward your third eye. Don't strain. Imagine an indigo light glowing between your eyebrows. Indigo is a color of serenity, transcendence, and transformation. As you sense this indigo light at your brow chakra, you may experience yourself moving beyond the limitations of ordinary, everyday thinking. Your inner vision may expand along with your ability to perceive deeper dimensions of your behavior or beliefs.

6 } Now call to mind the condition you wish to bring into your life. It may be something tangible, such as stopping smoking, or a shift in attitude, such as increasing your patience with other people. Feel the indigo light gently dissolving your resistance to releasing your old habit or behavior. Continue focusing on your brow chakra as you hold in your mind's eye an image of the outcome you desire. Allow yourself to see beyond your present situation. Perceive yourself liberated from the self-imposed limits of this habit or behavior. Feel what you would feel having become free of it.

7 } If you wish, gently press your fingertips to what Chinese medicine calls the Center of Power. This point is located at your solar plexus, about halfway between your belly button and the bottom of your breastbone. Continue applying light pressure to this point for about a minute, then release.

8 } Hold in your mind the image of the outcome you seek for as long as you can. Feel the joy, satisfaction, contentment, or whatever else you would feel when you are living the outcome. When you feel ready, mentally count from one to five. On the count of five, open your physical eyes.

Do this meditation daily until you've released the unwanted habit or behavior. After a while, your positive intentions will become ingrained and replace the old patterns. Repeat the meditation regularly as maintenance and to reinforce your newfound freedom from self-limiting beliefs.

THROW OFF THE WEIGHT OF DEPRESSION

According to a study conducted by Professor Mark Williams and his colleagues in the Department of Psychiatry at the University of Oxford, meditation can aid depression. The study, published in the journal *Behavior Research and Therapy* and reported in *ScienceDaily* in 2009, found that depressed patients who meditated in addition to receiving conventional treatment improved more than those who only received conventional treatment.

Depression results from the gradual buildup over time of little hurts, angers, fears, and so on that seem too trivial at the time to deal with, so you store them inside you. Eventually, without warning, they collapse upon you like a great weight . . . depression. Depression can last a few hours, a few days, or in the case of clinical depression, many years. The following meditation can lift depression effectively and quickly—often within a few days.

~~~~~~~~

1 } Sit or lie comfortably, with your eyes closed. Take a deep breath and exhale. Do this two more times. Relax using whichever method you prefer. Because you are in a state of depression, this may seem hard. Do the best you can.

2 } After you are somewhat relaxed, mentally count down from seven to one, relaxing more deeply with each count. On the count of one, find yourself sitting in a large, comfortable armchair.

3 } Sense a large sack of granulated substance (i.e., sand or salt) pressing down hard on your neck, chest, and thighs. Feel the weight, the heaviness, as this sack pushes against you. In the meditation, imagine it feels difficult to breathe.

4 } Notice a small penknife or nail file lying on the floor next to your chair. Reach down, pick up the penknife or nail file, and make a tiny incision no bigger than 1 inch (5 cm) at the base of the sack. (It is important that it be no bigger than 1 inch [5 cm].)

5 } As the sand slowly flows out, feel the sack gradually become less heavy and more flimsy. It is very important that you do this part of the meditation gradually (depression cannot be freed too quickly). Do not rush through it. Slowly and steadily, the grains pour out. As the sand slowly flows out and the sack becomes less and less heavy, you notice you can move your neck and shoulders. Feel the stiffness lessening. As the sand continues to flow out, your chest frees, allowing you to breathe more comfortably. Eventually, your abdomen opens, too.

6 } When most of the sand has run out and there is only about a pound (450 g) remaining, imagine yourself taking the loose sack and twirling it around until you've formed it into a long, twisted neck with a small, tight bulge of sand packed at the end.

7 } Envision yourself getting up from the chair and whirling the tightly wrapped sack around your head, like a lasso, then tossing it far into the distance. Be free of it. Now, still in meditation, imagine leaping high into the air, laughing, hooting, and going absolutely bonkers until you fall back into the chair, laughing. When you feel ready, mentally count from one to five. On the count of five, open your physical eyes and return.

Do this meditation only once per day for as long as it takes to lift the depression. It shouldn't take long. This meditation comes from Lazaris, an entity channeled through Jach Pursel. Martin has been attending Lazaris evenings and workshops for many years and finds these meditations to be among the most powerful he has experienced. For more information about Lazaris and the Lazaris material, go to www.lazaris.com.

CALM THE FEAR OF FLYING

In Martin's opinion, the only thing worse than flying is licorice—even though a study published in *American Scientist* in 2003 determined that the risk of being in an accident on an average domestic flight with a major U.S. airline is less than that involved in driving 10 miles (16 km) on an interstate highway in a rural area. And if you drive in an urban environment, you're more likely to have an accident in just 2 miles (3.2 km) than you would while flying in a commercial U.S. plane.

Like many other flying-phobic travelers, however, Martin experiences an anxiety disproportionate to the risk. For that reason, the following meditation is an important part of his personal repertoire. Each time he does this meditation, the plane trip turns out to be quite comfortable for him, despite the occasional bump or two.

1 } While sitting in your assigned seat on the plane, as other passengers are filing aboard, close your eyes and invite your Higher Self to sit beside you during the trip. (It doesn't matter who physically sits on either side of you.)

2 } While your eyes are closed, imagine you and your Higher Self forming a large, luminescent sphere of protection around you and the plane.

3 } Expand the sphere surrounding the plane so that it forms a luminescent tunnel extending from your plane's position at the gate all the way to your destination.

4 } Know that the plane you're on will be flying within this tunnel of protection for the entire time you are in the air, until you are safe on the ground at your destination.

Do this meditation each time you fly—you'll be amazed. (In case you're wondering, Martin is still working on a licorice meditation.)

DETOXIFY GRIEF AND RAGE

Many people repress fear, rage, shame, grief, despair, loneliness, and helplessness, instead of allowing themselves to feel the painful emotions. We do this because the emotions were too painful to feel at the time, or we were taught that feeling and expressing unpleasant emotions wasn't proper or socially acceptable. Or, maybe we believed if we ignored the feelings they would go away. However, attempting to ignore or deny unpleasant emotions produces a toxicity that can seriously impair normal physiological functioning. A review of studies linking cancer with anger, reported in *Cancer Nursing* in October 2000, noted that cancer patients often have extremely low anger scores. Evidence suggests "suppressed anger can be a precursor to the development of cancer, and also a factor in its progression after diagnosis."

Emotional and physical well-being require accessing all your emotions, pleasant or unpleasant. The following waking meditation lets you bring up repressed feelings and, once felt, release them. You can use this meditation to release any repressed emotion, but it is particularly effective for handling grief and rage.

~~~~~~

1 } After experiencing a situation where grief or rage would be the natural response, such as the loss of a loved one or a deep personal wounding—even years after such a loss or wounding—go to an isolated place where no one can hear or see you.

2 } Alone in this isolated place, close your eyes and allow the grief, rage, or other emotions to come up. It may take a couple of minutes. Even if you are currently in a good mood, choose to allow the deep feelings to surface. After a few minutes, perhaps sooner, you'll feel a welling up of emotion. Let it up and out, fully.

3 } Cry and wail, loudly. Scream and holler. Swear if you want to. Really feel it. Don't hold back. You are detoxing emotionally.

4 } The experience will most likely ebb and flow. Like vomiting, there will be periods of emotional "retching" and periods of calm. This is a natural part of the detoxing process.

5 } As you feel grief, waves of anger may surface as well. If you are grieving the loss of a loved one, for instance, feeling anger at the perceived abandonment is natural and human. It is nothing to be ashamed of. Feel this anger—don't stuff it down again. It's okay to be angry with your loved one.

(continued on page 78)

6 } If rage surfaces, scream and yell, but also do some physical detoxing. Get your body involved in the rage. Hit the bed or punch a pillow. Lie on your back and kick your feet; flail about, swinging your arms and legs wildly. The more you exert your body, the greater the detoxing.

7 } If you can't find an isolated, private place and you don't want others to hear you, cover your face with a pillow to muffle the screams. Or, pull your car off to the side of the road, close the windows, and just scream your head off.

This waking meditation should not go beyond ten minutes. Repeat it daily, even if you are in a good mood. When the grief and rage are fully out of your system, you'll sense a wonderful lightness and serenity. You will be at peace with your loss, and free of the rage.

QUIET THE VOICE OF FEAR

In a study to examine meditation's effects on quality of life, reported in *General Hospital Psychiatry* magazine in 2001, participants meditated twenty minutes per day for eight weeks. At the end of the trial, their test results showed a 38 percent reduction in psychological distress and a 44 percent decrease in anxiety. A year later, those who meditated continued to exhibit improved mental and physical well-being.

Fear, like pain, is a messenger. Pain tells us something physical needs attention; fear tells us something emotional needs attention. If we can honor our fears by feeling them—without letting ourselves be overwhelmed by them—at the proper time and place, we can heal and release them. Fear is not the enemy. Pushing it down or denying it is what causes problems. Just as numbing your body with painkillers so you won't feel pain could be physically dangerous, refusing to feel and release fear can also be unwise. Instead of trying to "kill the messenger," use this meditation to face your fear, forgive it, and let it go.

~~~~~~~~

1 } Sit or lie comfortably, with your eyes closed. Take a deep breath and exhale. Do this two more times. Relax using whichever method you prefer. After you are somewhat relaxed, mentally count down from seven to one, relaxing more deeply with each count.

2 } On the count of one, find yourself in your Safe Place. Use your inner sense(s) to make this place more real to you. Sense the beauty, love, blessed solitude, or enchantment of this place. If you wish, you can invite your Higher Self to join you.

3 } Invite your fear to present itself to you. It may be a current fear or an old one still lingering from your past. It may appear to you in a personified form, or maybe as a younger part of yourself (perhaps you as a child or an adolescent, who originally experienced this fear). See or sense the personified fear or younger version of you.

4 } Allow the fear to speak. Remember, its fear is your fear. It may tell you why it's fearful. It may weep, wail, cry out in anger, or react in some other way. Or, you may sense nothing but the fear itself. Listen. Feel it. Empathize with it.

5 } When it's done, when it can't speak anymore, hold it, love it, reassure it. Lovingly tell it, "You'll be fine. I will not abandon you." Remember, love is stronger than fear.

6 } Sense it becoming more relaxed and at peace. Soon, it fades away.

7 } Now, close your mental eyes and mentally count from one to five. On the count of five, open your physical eyes. Your fear will be gone or greatly lessened.

(continued on page 80)

Do this meditation each day until the fear is healed. If you feel fear, anxiety, or any other negative emotion at a time when it is inappropriate to work with it, such as in a business meeting or at a special social event, ask your Higher Self to lift the fear from you. You will work with it later. You should feel better immediately. Later that day or evening, sit down and ask your Higher Self to bring the fear back. When it returns and you feel it, do the above meditation.

PUT AN END TO SHAME

Shame is a painful feeling of self-condemnation that accompanies the erroneous belief that you are inherently defective or unworthy. It is linked with cultural, religious, and/or familial opinions and conditioning. In extreme cases, shame can lead to illness, substance abuse, depression, aggressive behavior, and other problems. The following meditation helps you remove the stigma of shame, so it doesn't limit your well-being.

~~~~~~~

1 } Sit or lie comfortably, with your eyes closed. Take a deep breath and exhale. Do this two more times. Relax using whichever method you prefer. Bring to mind something about which you feel shame. Imagine your shame as a colored patch, stuck someplace on your body. The color should be one that you find dull or ugly.

2 } Now, think of something else about which you feel shame. Imagine this as another ugly-colored patch stuck on your body. Repeat this procedure with as many incidents of shame as you choose to address at this time.

3 } When you see or sense a number of colored patches on your skin, notice that these patches are like translucent scales and as thin as onion skin. Notice also that these patches have been applied to your skin by someone else.

4 } Touch one of the patches and notice that you can easily pull it off. Peel away the colored patch. Crumple it between your fingers and observe how easily it disintegrates.

5 } Feel a sensation of relief, comfort, joy, lightness, or something else now that the ugly patch has been removed. Do the same thing to another patch. Continue in this manner until you've pulled off all the ugly-colored patches.

6 } Now, look at your skin, free of the patches. Observe yourself without the overlays of your own or someone else's negative judgment.

7 } Spend a few moments enjoying feelings of relief, serenity, clarity, joy, and self-acceptance. When you are ready, open your eyes.

Do this meditation regularly, for at least ten or fifteen minutes at a time, to release feelings of shame. Over time, you'll notice fewer and fewer colored patches on your skin. Eventually, they'll all disappear entirely.

RIDE THE WAVES TO BALANCE MOOD SWINGS

A seven-week study of the effects of meditation, done at the University of Calgary in Alberta, Canada (published in *Supportive Care in Cancer* in 2001), examined emotional distress and mood disturbances in cancer patients. Eighty-nine patients, male and female, with various types and degrees of disease meditated as a group in a clinical setting and did at-home meditation on an individual basis. Researchers found that distress diminished among the patients during the study and remained lower six months later in a follow-up.

Whether mood swings are due to external or internal circumstances, meditation can help bring your emotions into balance. The following technique lets you see ups and downs as part of life, and guides you to "go with the flow."

1 } Sit or lie comfortably, with your eyes closed. Take a deep breath and exhale. Do this two more times. Relax using whichever method you prefer.

2 } Bring to mind an image of the ocean. Include as much sensory detail in the scene as possible. See the sun shining on the water; smell the salt-scented air; hear the roar of the ocean and the sound of the waves breaking on the shore.

3 } Now, imagine you are floating in the ocean, riding the waves. (If you prefer, put yourself on a surfboard or small boat.) Water is a symbol for the emotions. The waves represent the various events and experiences in life. The waves roll by, one by one, in a steady pattern, just as life's ups and downs come and go.

4 } Feel yourself floating up and down as the waves roll beneath you. Relax and let the ocean carry you along. Notice that it is just as pleasant to slide down into the trough as it is to rise up to the crest. Notice that neither the up nor the down part of the cycle is more difficult. Relax and let the ocean buoy you.

5 } Observe your ability to ride the waves and to handle the ups and downs equally. Continue floating on the waves for as long as you like.

6 } When you're ready, allow the waves to bring you gently to shore.

7 } Open your eyes.

Do this meditation during periods of emotional stress or life challenges. It will help balance your emotions and keep you from overreacting to incidents in your daily life.

HEAL THE LOSS OF A LOVED ONE

The loss of a loved one is the most devastating time in our lives. Be it a family member, a spouse, a friend, or an animal companion, the loss is something we never totally get over— nor should we. But we can, and should, move beyond it. What makes human love so unique and magnificent is that, in spite of loss, we do not give up our pursuit of loving. We stand up, brush ourselves off, and love again.

It's important that we not cut ourselves off from our humanness by misusing grief. If we deny our grief and stuff it deep inside, we dishonor our loved ones and ourselves. If we wear it as a "Red Badge of Martyrdom," wallowing in it, grief becomes a display rather than a valued ritual of love.

The following meditation helps you not only honor and heal your loss, but it also lets you move beyond grief, with the loving aid of your departed one. Remember, your loved one is gone, but never lost.

~~~~~

1 } Sit or lie comfortably, with your eyes closed. Take a deep breath and exhale. Do this two more times. Relax as best you can, using which-ever method you prefer. After you are somewhat relaxed, mentally count down from seven to one, relaxing more deeply with each count.

2 } On the count of one, find yourself in your Safe Place. Take time to feel the beauty, love, blessed solitude, or enchantment of this place. It is especially important that you feel loved here.

3 } If you want to, and only if you want to, invite your Higher Self to join you. Sit together. Love together. If you want to, and only if you want to, let your Higher Self hold you. It is your call; do whatever feels most comfortable for you.

4 } Now, invite your departed loved one to join you in your Safe Place. Your loved one will come and be with you. He/she will have a radiant glow about him/her. Your loved one is now more of his/her truer self than he/she ever was in physical life. If you are willing, you can sense this.

5 } Be together. Talk together. Express all your feelings to your loved one. Hold nothing back. Express and feel your pain, anger, or sense of abandonment or betrayal if that is what you feel. Express it all. It's okay. Your loved one understands and will help you. Your loved one will want to communicate with you as well. He/she may tell you why he/she left. He/she may express feelings he/she couldn't share with you while in physical form. He/she may want to apologize for his/her negligence. Remember, your loved one is different now. Healing can happen between you here (if you want that).

6} Sit together. If you want to, and only if you want to, let your departed loved one hold you. Grieve now. Let it flow freely. Know you can always return and be with your loved one again in this way, anytime you choose.

7} When you are ready, close your mental eyes, and mentally count from one to five. On the count of five, open your physical eyes and return.

Don't rush immediately into activity. Take as long as you need before returning to your normal routine. Be aware that grief will continue to surface for as long as is necessary for its healing. Honor it, feel it, and let it flow. Grief is a part of your human heart's experience. Respect it. Repeat this meditation as often as you wish or feel is necessary.

"We know stress is a contributor to all the major modern killers," points out Charles L. Raison, MD. By reducing stress, meditation can not only improve your quality of life but also can extend your life. Two studies, reported in the *American Journal of Cardiology,* in 2005, followed more than 200 men and women for up to eighteen years and found that those who practiced meditation had a 23 percent lower death rate during that time period than their non-meditating peers.

MEDITATIONS FOR
OVERALL HEALTH, REJUVENATION, AND LONGEVITY

USE THE BREATH OF FIRE TO TAP VITAL ENERGY

Meditation is a core ingredient of yoga. The two disciplines function together hand in hand. The following practice comes from the Kundalini school of yoga, which emphasizes breathing and meditation to tap vital energy (called prana) located at the base of the spine. This dynamic breathing meditation, known as the "Breath of Fire," draws latent energy up through your entire body to provide a quick "pick-me-up," physically and mentally.

~~~~~

1 } Sit in a position that is comfortable for you— you don't have to sit in the traditional, cross-legged lotus posture. Take a deep breath, inhaling through your nose, letting the breath fill and expand your stomach, then your chest. Exhale through your nose, pulling your stomach in toward your spine until you've expelled all the air from your lungs.

2 } Inhale again, and exhale half the air. Exhale the rest of the air quickly through your nose with a snort. As you exhale, simultaneously pull your stomach in toward your spine.

3 } Relax your stomach muscles and immediately inhale with a sharp sniff. Don't pause between inhaling and exhaling. In-breaths and out-breaths should be equal. You may find it easier to focus on the exhalation, coordinating your out-breath with the act of pulling in your stomach. (You'll naturally inhale when you release your stomach muscles.)

4 } Don't worry about speed. Concentrate on keeping your breath steady and rhythmic. Pull your stomach in as you exhale, and relax your stomach muscles as you inhale. Continue a rhythmic pumping motion with your breath, as if your body were a bellows. (This breathing technique is sometimes called "bellows breath.")

5 } Keep your mind focused on your breathing. If thoughts arise into your consciousness, simply let them go and return your attention to your breath.

6 } In the beginning, spend about thirty seconds at a time breathing in this manner (stop if you start to feel dizzy or otherwise uncomfortable). Work up to two minutes or longer if you feel capable of doing so without discomfort.

It may take a few attempts before it becomes easy and natural for you to perform this unique breathing practice. Do the Breath of Fire meditation any time you feel lethargic and need an energy boost, or when you seek to improve mental clarity and focus.

CONNECT WITH THE SOURCE OF ALL LIFE

You are not alone. You have never been alone. You will never be alone. You are part of a multidimensional matrix that links all of us—humans, animals, plants, deities, and other nonphysical entities—to one another, and to the rest of the universe. As French anthropologist, priest, philosopher, and mystic Pierre Teilhard de Chardin explained, "We are spiritual beings having a human experience."

A 1998 review in the American Medical Association's *Archives of Family Medicine* noted that spiritual commitment may help people prevent, cope with, and recover from mental and physical illness. One of the shortest and most powerful statements is "I Am." This meditation affirms your spiritual existence, your eternal nature that continues even when the physical body dies, and your connection to all that is.

1 } Sit, stand, or lie in a place where you feel safe and comfortable. Close your eyes, and relax using whichever method you prefer.

2 } Begin breathing slowly and deeply, growing more calm and serene with each breath. Focus your attention on your breathing as you allow all mundane thoughts to slip away. Realize the air you breathe gives life to you and all creatures on Earth. You and all creatures breathe the same air. It envelops our planet and connects us to one another.

3 } As you exhale, say the words "I Am." Feel your head, throat, and chest resonate with the sounds "I Am." As you speak these words, become aware of your link with the divine realm.

4 } Sense life energy flowing in through your crown chakra (at the top of your head) and down into your body. Inhale again and sense the breath of life connecting you with all beings on Earth. Exhale again as you intone the words "I Am."

5 } Feel the sound expand beyond your head, throat, and chest until it resonates through your entire body. Witness yourself as the spiritual being you are. Know that you are this spiritual being, not your body or your mind. Feel your link with the universe and all that is eternal.

6 } Continue breathing and chanting in this manner for as long as you wish.

7 } When you feel ready, open your eyes. Breathe as you normally do, but retain your awareness of your spiritual nature and your connection with all that is.

Do this meditation regularly, for a minimum of five minutes at a time, to remember who you truly are.

BALANCE HORMONAL FUNCTION TO SLOW AGING

Dehydroepiandrosterone sulfate (DHEA-S), the adrenal androgen sometimes called the "youth hormone," is associated with aging as well as health in general. DHEA-S levels decrease as a result of stress, illness, and aging, and low DHEA-S levels correlate with cardiovascular disease and breast cancer. Dr. Jay Glaser, a Massachusetts MD and Ayurvedic doctor, and Dr. Deepak Chopra studied nearly 1,800 people to see how meditation affected their hormonal function. The doctors found that subjects who meditated had significantly higher levels of DHEA-S—comparable to people five to ten years younger—than non-meditators.

Other studies, such as those reported in the journal *Psychosomatic Medicine* in 1986, indicate that meditation can also lower levels of the stress hormone cortisol. Researchers at Stanford University showed that unbalanced cortisol can predict early death in women with breast cancer. The following meditation helps balance hormonal function to keep you younger and healthier longer.

The process enables you to integrate all aspects of yourself, so you become more creative, self-aware, and fulfilled.

~~~~~

1 } Lie on your back in a place where you feel comfortable and close your eyes. Relax using whichever method you prefer. Turn your attention to your breathing as you empty your mind of all thoughts.

2 } Breathe slowly, deeply, allowing yourself to relax further. As you inhale, imagine oxygen entering your body through the sole of your left foot. Feel the oxygen flowing up your left leg, into your abdomen, and crossing your body at your heart. The oxygen continues up to your right shoulder and arm, up your neck, and into your head.

3 } As you exhale, imagine carbon dioxide flowing down your neck, then your left shoulder and arm, and crossing your body at your heart. Feel it continue down into your abdomen, then your right leg, and leave your body through the sole of your right foot.

4 } The pattern your breath makes as it flows through your body is similar to the crossed ribbons worn to signify support for cancer research and other causes.

5 } Continue breathing in this manner, keeping your attention focused on the movement of your breath through your body. Sense your system becoming balanced, strengthened, and renewed.

6 } If thoughts intrude into your awareness, simply let them go and bring your attention back to your breathing.

7 } Continue in this manner for as long as you like. When you feel ready, open your eyes.

Practice this meditation regularly, for at least ten minutes at a time, to balance your hormonal function, reduce stress, and improve your overall health and well-being.

SWIM THROUGH LIFE'S CHALLENGES

A study of more than 40,000 men over a period of thirty-two years, published in *Medical News Today* in 2009, showed that swimming contributes significantly to longevity. Dr. Steven Blair, professor at the University of South Carolina, who led the study, compared swimmers with runners, walkers, and sedentary people and determined that "swimmers had the lowest death rate." The University of Indiana's Dr. Joel M. Stager, who has also studied swimming and aging, says, "Exercising in water slows down the aging process, and often quite dramatically—by upwards of 20 percent in some cases."

Swimming requires a combination of effort and relaxation. To stay afloat, you must cease struggling and allow the water to buoy you. The same concept can be applied to life. If you struggle, you'll go under. But if you relax and allow the universe to hold you up, you can glide through life's challenges. Instead of swimming purely for exercise, use swimming as an active meditation—you'll enhance the healthful benefits of both.

1 } At the edge of a lake, a pool, or the ocean, take a few moments to reflect upon the healing nature of water. The human body is composed largely of water, so you already have an affinity with water. Calm and center yourself before you enter the water.

2 } As you step into the water, imagine it as symbolizing the universe or the collective unconscious of which you are a part. Feel your connection with the water and what it represents. Feel it embrace you as you lower yourself into it.

3 } As you relax and begin to float, allow yourself to appreciate the water and its uplifting power. It will buoy you even if you don't do a thing but lie on your back. Notice how the water gently caresses your skin, soothing and refreshing you. Sense the water cleansing you of all tension, anxiety, and discomfort.

4 } Begin swimming, using whichever stroke you prefer. Swim at a slow, relaxed, steady pace. Feel the peaceful sensation of gliding easily through the water. Keep your attention focused on each stroke you take, letting all other thoughts slip away from your mind.

5 } Experience your muscles working harmoniously to propel you smoothly and pleasantly through the water. Let the rhythm of your motions balance your mind and body, producing a sense of harmony and serenity.

6 } Be aware of the water's power to keep you afloat. Notice the ease with which you move through it. Similarly, the universe's power will keep you afloat regardless of the difficulties you may be experiencing in your life—all you have to do is stop struggling and allow it to support you. Imagine you are gliding through life as easily as you are swimming through the water.

7} If unwanted thoughts intrude, let them float away and turn your attention back to your strokes. Continue swimming for as long as you like.

8} When you're ready, emerge from the lake, pool, or ocean feeling refreshed and rejuvenated.

Do this meditation as often as you like, for as long as is comfortable for you.

REJUVENATE YOUR SKIN

According to the American Society for Aesthetic Plastic Surgery, more than ten million surgical and nonsurgical cosmetic procedures were performed in 2008. Before you undergo costly treatments, try this quick and easy meditation. It allows you to collect healing energy in your hands and direct it to your face—or any other part of your body that requires rejuvenation.

1 } Sit, stand, or lie in a place where you feel safe and comfortable. Close your eyes, and relax using whichever method you prefer.

2 } Press your palms together and rub them vigorously for a few moments, until you feel them growing warm.

3 } Stop rubbing your palms and hold them open, toward your chin, about 1 inch (5 cm) away from your face. Slowly move your hands upward from your chin to the top of your head. Feel the rejuvenating energy radiating from your palms onto your face. Imagine wrinkles, acne, or other blemishes disappearing as you direct healing energy into your skin.

4 } When you get to the top of your head, flick your hands as if you were throwing off water.

5 } Again, rub your palms together for a few moments until they feel warm.

6 } Holding your palms about 1 inch (5 cm) away from your face, again move your hands up slowly from your chin to the top of your head. When you get to the top of your head, flick your hands as if you were throwing off water.

7 } Repeat for a total of six times, or until you feel you've accomplished your objective. When you are ready, open your eyes.

Spend a few minutes each morning and each night performing this practive. You can focus rejuvenating energy to any part of your body using the same method. Remember to visualize your body as being completely healthy, youthful, and perfect in every way.

CHARGE YOUR CHAKRAS TO BOOST VITALITY

Chakra is a Sanskrit word meaning "wheel." These vortices of light, which align roughly along your backbone from the base of the spine to the top of your head, possess great power and influence over all aspects of your life: physical, mental, emotional, spiritual, and behavioral. The human body has seven major chakras, or energy centers, and each corresponds to a particular region of the body. They also affect and are affected by seven principal life areas: safety and security, pleasure and enjoyment, emotions, love and self-love, communication and expression, subtle sensing or intuition, and spirituality.

When the chakras become depleted due to fatigue, overuse, illness, emotional or mental problems, and so on, your health, vitality, and general well-being decline. Just as a battery can lose its charge with overuse, the chakras can lose their charge from misuse. This meditation recharges them.

～～～～～

1 } Sit or lie comfortably, with your eyes closed. Take a deep breath and exhale. Do this two more times. Relax using whichever method you prefer. After you are somewhat relaxed, mentally count down from seven to one, relaxing more deeply with each count.

2 } On the count of one, find yourself in your Safe Place at evening time (evening in the meditation). You will find your Higher Self waiting, standing by a "healing bed." This could be a soft bed of flowers, downy feathers, sheets of silk or satin, or whatever appears to you. The space is illuminated by candlelight and surrounded by crystals. Let whatever appears, appear. This healing place is comfortable, beautiful, enchanting, magical, and loving. Lie down upon the healing bed. Your Higher Self sits beside you. Close your mental eyes.

3 } Bring your attention to your tailbone region. What should appear here as a sphere of bright, shiny red is, instead, a dull and distorted color. Mentally spin the sphere in whichever direction is easiest. Start slowly and gradually increase the speed. Spin the sphere faster and faster. As you spin the sphere it becomes more and more red. When it is a vibrant red, begin to decrease the spinning. When it becomes very slow, stop the spinning and hold the energy there for a few seconds.

4 } Bring your attention, now, to the genital region. What should appear here as a sphere of bright, juicy orange is, instead, a dull and distorted color. Mentally spin the sphere in whichever direction is easiest. Start slowly and gradually increase the speed. Spin the sphere faster and faster. As you spin the sphere it becomes more and more orange. When it is a vibrant, juicy

orange, begin to decrease the spinning. When it becomes very slow, stop the spinning and hold the energy there for a few seconds.

5 } Bring your attention, now, to the navel region. What should appear here as a sphere of bright, buttery yellow is, instead, a dull and distorted color. Mentally spin the sphere in whichever direction is easiest. Start slowly and gradually increase the speed. Spin the sphere faster and faster. As you spin the sphere it becomes more and more yellow. When it is a vibrant, buttery yellow begin to decrease the spinning. When it becomes very slow, stop the spinning and hold the energy there for a few seconds.

6 } Bring your attention, now, to the heart region. What should appear here as a sphere of bright, emerald green is, instead, a dull and distorted color. Mentally spin the sphere in whichever direction is easiest. Start slowly and gradually increase the speed. Spin the sphere faster and faster. As you spin the sphere it becomes more and more green. When it is a vibrant emerald green, begin to decrease the spinning. When it becomes very slow, stop the spinning and hold the energy there for a few seconds.

7 } Bring your attention, now, to the throat region. What should appear here as a sphere of bright sapphire blue is, instead, a dull and distorted color. Mentally spin the sphere in whichever direction is easiest. Start slowly and gradually increase the speed. Spin the sphere faster and faster. As you spin the sphere it becomes more and more blue. When it is a vibrant sapphire blue, begin to decrease the spinning. When it becomes very slow, stop the spinning and hold the energy there for a few seconds.

8 } Bring your attention, now, to the third eye region. What should appear here as a sphere of brilliant indigo is, instead, a dull and distorted color. Mentally spin the sphere in whichever direction is easiest. Start slowly and gradually increase the speed. Spin the sphere faster and faster. As you spin the sphere it becomes more and more indigo. When it is a vibrant indigo, begin to decrease the spinning. When it becomes very slow, stop the spinning and hold the energy there for a few seconds.

9 } Bring your attention, now, to the crown of your head. What should appear here as a sphere of bright, beautiful violet is, instead, a dull and distorted color. Mentally spin the sphere in whichever direction is easiest. Start slowly and gradually increase the speed. Spin the sphere faster and faster. As you spin the sphere it becomes more and more violet. When it is a vibrant violet, begin to decrease the spinning. When it becomes very slow, stop the spinning and hold the energy there for a few seconds.

10 } Your chakras are now fully charged. When you feel ready, mentally count from one to five. On the count of five, open your physical eyes and return.

We recommend doing this meditation regularly, at least once a month, to keep your chakras charged and functioning optimally.

ERASE NEGATIVE THINKING TO ENHANCE HEALTH AND LONGEVITY

"Happier people live longer," proclaimed an article published in *U.S. News and World Report* in 2006, based on nearly a dozen clinical studies of how attitude affects health. The studies showed that optimistic people are less likely to experience heart attacks, strokes, arthritis, and other debilitating physical conditions. The same year, Carnegie Mellon researchers also found that people with positive outlooks contracted fewer colds and flus than their more pessimistic counterparts.

Maybe Bobby McFerrin was on to something when he sang, "Don't Worry, Be Happy." The following ongoing meditation helps you become aware of your negative thoughts so you can transform them into positive ones.

1 } Make a commitment to change unhealthy thought patterns. You have the power to control your emotions with your thoughts, and you can shift unpleasant feelings to happier ones by making a conscious decision to adjust your thinking. Start paying attention to your thoughts and feelings.

2 } Each time you notice yourself feeling anxious, angry, fearful, sad, discouraged, or otherwise unhappy—in the absence of any immediate, strong, and reasonable impetus—stop what you're doing and turn your attention to the feeling.

3 } What were you thinking right before you experienced the negative emotion? Retrace your thoughts until you can connect your emotional reaction(s) to a particular thought(s). Close your eyes and bring to mind the thought that triggered your unpleasant emotional reaction. Imagine the negative thought written on a blackboard.

4 } See or sense yourself picking up an eraser and erasing the thought from the blackboard. Acknowledge your power over the thought and your ability to wipe it out, so it no longer impacts your happiness and well-being. Notice how erasing this idea makes you feel.

5 } Now, shift your focus to something more positive—a memory of a pleasant experience, an image of a loved one or a pet, or another thought that makes you happy just thinking about it. Notice how bringing to mind a positive memory or image shifts your emotions into a lighter, happier place.

6 } Enjoy this positive feeling for as long as you choose. When you're ready, take a deep breath and open your eyes.

7 } Each time a negative thought arises into your awareness, repeat this process.

This ongoing meditation requires vigilance and dedication, because we've grown accustomed to letting our minds wander to—and wallow in—negative thought patterns. The hardest part of this meditation may be catching negative thoughts when they first intrude into your consciousness. It gets easier, though—you'll soon train yourself to stop dwelling on unpleasant, harmful ideas and instead enjoy positive, uplifting ones. *Note:* This doesn't mean denying and repressing legitimate feelings; it simply suggests paying attention to your thoughts and choosing to discard those that don't serve you or your intentions.

USE COLOR TO TUNE AND HEAL YOUR BODY

Back in 1942, Russian scientist S. V. Krakov showed that color measurably affects the nervous system. He conducted experiments on test subjects and discovered red stimulated the sympathetic portion of the autonomic nervous system, whereas blue affected the parasympathetic. The sympathetic division governs body functions related to the need for quick action and immediate responses, whereas the parasympathetic governs those that don't require immediate responses. Since then, numerous researchers have studied the healing benefits of chromatherapy. In 2009, *ScienceDaily* reported that simply shining blue light on two common strains of methicillin-resistant Staphylococcus aureus killed more than 90 percent of the staph.

The following meditation uses color to tap your mind's innate healing ability. If you wish, you can physically shine colored light on your body as well to enhance the mental imagery and healing.

~~~~~

1 } Sit or lie comfortably, with your eyes closed. Take a deep breath and exhale. Do this two more times. Relax using whichever method you prefer. After you are somewhat relaxed, mentally count down from seven to one, relaxing more deeply with each count.

2 } On the count of one, find yourself in your Safe Place. Feel the beauty, love, blessed solitude, or enchantment of this place.

3 } Select a color that suits your purposes. If you wish to lower your blood pressure, reduce inflammation, or calm nervous tension, choose blue or indigo. If you want to stimulate energy or strengthen your body, use red or orange. Green stabilizes and balances your entire system. See or sense light of the color you've chosen shining on your body. The light is clear, radiant, and beautiful.

4 } You may direct the colored light to a particular part of your body that needs healing or balancing. Or, if you prefer, imagine you are completely surrounded by a large sphere of colored light. Feel the colored light gently working on your body, aligning, toning, and healing whatever ails you. Sense the light not only shining on you but also suffusing your body. Feel it flowing through you, healing you inside and out.

5 } Enjoy the pleasant sensation. If you've selected blue or indigo light, feel a soothing coolness washing over and through you. If you've chosen red or orange, experience its comfortable warmth glowing around and within you. When you feel you've gleaned as much as you need from this colored light, you can choose to work with another color or another part of your body if you wish.

6 } Repeat this process, again directing the colored light where you need it. If your intention is to balance and tone your entire system, see or sense yourself surrounded by each color of the spectrum, one color at a time, beginning with red and ending with violet.

7 } Continue in this manner for as long as you like. When you feel ready, mentally count from one to five.

8 } On the count of five, open your physical eyes and return.

Do the following meditation at least once a month to maintain optimal health. If you are working with a particular problem or condition, perform the meditation twice daily for fifteen to twenty minutes per session.

Can meditation boost your brain power? Sara Lazar, PhD, a research scientist at Massachusetts General Hospital, found that regular meditation can actually increase the size of some parts of the brain. Size may also correlate with mental performance. A two-year study of one hundred college students, published in *ScienceDaily*, showed meditation improved their IQ scores.

MEDITATIONS TO IMPROVE CONCENTRATION, MEMORY, AND MENTAL CLARITY

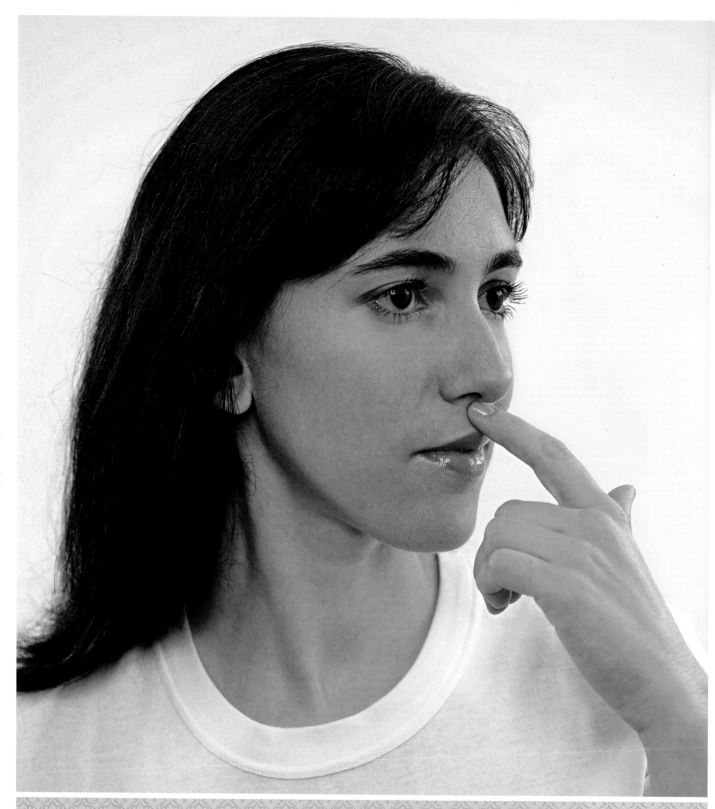

INCREASE MENTAL CLARITY AND ATTENTION

Since 1992, Richard J. Davidson, PhD, director of the Laboratory for Affective Neuroscience at the University of Wisconsin, and his colleagues have studied the effects of meditation on complex mental processes. Working in collaboration with the Dalai Lama and Tibetan monks, researchers found that meditation strengthens the part of the brain that enables us to pay attention. "Attention is the key to learning, and meditation helps you voluntarily regulate it," says Davidson.

The following meditation incorporates acupressure to enhance benefits. Use it to promote mental clarity, deepen concentration, and improve your ability to pay attention.

1 } Sit in a comfortable place, with your eyes closed. Take a deep breath and exhale. Do this two more times. Relax using whichever method you prefer.

2 } Continue breathing slowly, deeply, and rhythmically. Keep your attention focused on your breathing.

3 } Whenever a thought arises into your awareness or your mind starts to wander, gently press your index finger to the small depression between your upper lip and the tip of your nose. Hold this acupressure point for a few moments as you release the thought from your mind.

4 } Return your attention to your breathing. Each time a thought intrudes into your awareness, press this point and hold it until the thought slips away.

5 } Notice your mind growing more and more relaxed.

6 } Gradually, your meditation will deepen and thoughts will become less frequent.

7 } Continue in this manner for as long as you like. When you feel ready, open your eyes.

Do this meditation regularly, for ten minutes or more at a time, to clear the "cobwebs" from your mind. Throughout the day, whenever you need to recall something or wish to sharpen your attention, simply close your eyes, take a deep breath, and press this acupressure point for a few moments.

STOP MULTITASKING TO IMPROVE YOUR MEMORY

As we age, many of us experience memory decline. However, a study of seventy-three elderly individuals (with a mean age of eighty-one), published in 1989 in the *Journal of Personality and Social Psychology*, found that meditation helps reverse age-related memory loss. Study participants who practiced meditation scored higher than the control group when tested for word fluency, cognitive flexibility, and other mental skills.

In our fast-paced society, we often multitask. When we try to do more than one thing at a time, we only partly pay attention to what we're doing. Meditation, says Dr. Jon Kabat-Zinn, founder of the Stress Reduction Clinic at the University of Massachusetts Medical Center, is "about allowing yourself to be where you already are." The following active meditation improves memory by training your brain to pay attention and focus on one thing at a time.

~~~~~~

1 } Choose a simple, mundane task such as folding laundry, washing dishes, or weeding the garden. Do only one thing at a time. Don't talk on the phone while you're folding the laundry, for instance.

2 } Put your full attention on your task. Set all other considerations aside for the time being. Be fully present in each moment, instead of letting your mind jump about to thoughts of the future or the past.

3 } Observe things you might not normally notice—the temperature of the dishwater, for example, or the textures of the clothes you're folding. Bring all your senses into play. If you're gardening, smell the flowers, hear the birds singing. Feel the sun on your back, the breeze on your face as you pull weeds. See the small details, such as the rainbows in soap bubbles or the buttons on a blouse.

4 } Take your time, instead of rushing through the job.

5 } Admire the skill your fingers possess. Take pleasure in your ability to perform this everyday task.

6 } Whenever your mind starts to wander, bring it back gently to the task before you.

7 } By the time you've completed the chore, you'll feel calmer and more relaxed.

Apply this method to other tasks as well. See every chore as an opportunity to practice meditation. Not only will your memory begin to improve, but you may also feel that you have more time—not less.

COMBINE CHANTING AND MUDRAS TO IMPROVE CONCENTRATION

Sara Lazar, PhD, a research scientist at Massachusetts General Hospital, examined the effects of meditation on decision making, attention, and memory. The study, reported in *Time* magazine in 2006, found that the cerebral cortex (which governs these mental functions) was thicker in subjects who meditated daily. Meditation also slowed thinning of the cerebral cortex, which usually happens as we age.

The following meditation, known as "Kirtan Kriya," combines a simple chant with finger mudras. Mudras are gestures used to guide energy flow to the body and mind. In some cases, they activate acupressure points, particularly in the hands and fingers, to generate specific results. By enhancing the body-mind-spirit connection, Kirtan Kriya improves concentration, mental clarity, and focus. The Sanskrit chant used in this meditation—*Sa Ta Na Ma*—translates as birth, life, death, rebirth.

1 } Sit in a position you find comfortable. If you choose to sit cross-legged, rest your hands, palms up, on your knees. If that isn't comfortable for you, sit in a chair and rest your hands, palms up, on your thighs or the arms of the chair. Close your eyes and begin breathing slowly and deeply, paying attention to your breath.

2 } When you feel relaxed, press the tip of your right thumb to your right index fingertip, and the tip of your left thumb to your left index fingertip. Say aloud "Sa." (You needn't think about the meanings of the Sanskrit sounds—your subconscious mind will absorb them and comprehend the cycle of continuity they denote.)

3 } Next, press the tip of your right thumb to your right middle fingertip, and the tip of your left thumb to your left middle fingertip. Say aloud "Ta."

4 } Press the tip of your right thumb to your right ring fingertip, and the tip of your left thumb to your left ring fingertip. Say aloud "Na."

5 } Press the tip of your right thumb to your right pinkie fingertip, and the tip of your left thumb to your left pinkie fingertip. Say aloud "Ma."

6 } Continue chanting while pressing your fingers and thumbs together in a rhythmic manner, again and again. Activating the acupressure points in your fingertips triggers energy reflexes in the brain. The sounds and repetition calm, center, and focus your mind.

7 } Continue doing this for as long as you like. When you feel ready, stop and return your attention to your breathing. Open your eyes.

CREATE A MANDALA TO PROMOTE MENTAL BALANCE

Mandalas are elaborate, circular images that symbolize the world. The word *mandala* means "circle" in Sanskrit. In some mandalas, the top hemisphere represents the heavens, the lower hemisphere the earth, signifying the interconnection between the two levels of existence. Although mandalas are often painted, they can be fashioned of any material. Many contain archetypal, spiritual, or magical motifs, as well as personal ones.

Traditional Hindu and Buddhist mandalas may include the figures of deities, *devas* (nature spirits), and bodhisattvas in their designs, with the god or goddess to whom the mandala is dedicated positioned at the center. In Tibetan Buddhism, these patterns are used to aid meditation. Your mandala should contain whatever symbols, colors, and images appeal to or have meaning for you.

1 } Collect materials you'll need to create your mandala: paper and paste, paints and brushes, crayons or colored markers, magazine pictures, fabric, and so on.

2 } Put all other thoughts out of your mind for the time being, and focus on your task. The act of creating a mandala is a meditation in itself.

3 } Draw a circle, as large as you like. Within the circle, sketch, paint, paste, sew, or otherwise combine images that you find appealing. You may wish to keep the image of the world or the universe in mind. The upper portion of the circle might represent the sky, the lower part the earth. Or, the upper half could symbolize the conscious mind and the outer world, the lower half the inner, subconscious dimension

4 } As you fashion your mandala, imbue it with intention—it becomes an embodiment of your vision, feelings, and objectives.

5 } When you've finished, you can use the mandala as a tool for meditation. Instead of forming images in your mind, as you would during creative visualization practices, relax and gaze at the mandala. Without analysis or judgment, observe the individual images and the mandala as a whole. Notice details. Try to see beyond the obvious. See the whole as more than the sum of its parts. Pay attention to any insights or impressions that arise into your awareness.

6 } Reflect on your mandala whenever you like, for as long as you like.

If you prefer, place the completed mandala in a spot where you will see it often, so that its meaning becomes impressed on your subconscious.

UTILIZE MORE OF YOUR BRAIN

Scientists estimate we use only 5 to 15 percent of our brains. This idea is often attributed to William James, who wrote an article in 1908 titled "The Energies of Man." Actually, we are using 100 percent of our brains, but we're aware of only 5 to 15 percent. Increasing your mental potential involves improving analytical and intuitive thinking, as well as expanding awareness and perception.

Three controlled trials of Taiwanese students (published in the journal *Intelligence* in 2001) measured the effects of meditation on cognitive, emotional, and perceptual functioning. The study showed that meditation increased the students' IQs, as well as their creativity, practical intelligence (adapting to, shaping, and functioning in your environment), and fluid intelligence (the ability to problem solve and reason abstractly).

Meditation heightens mental functioning by balancing your right brain (which controls intuition and creativity) and your left brain (which governs logic, analysis, and rational thinking), enabling you to utilize more of your gray matter.

~~~~~~

1 } Sit or lie comfortably, with your eyes closed. Take a deep breath and exhale. Do this two more times. Relax using whichever method you prefer. After you are relaxed, mentally count down from seven to one, relaxing more deeply with each count.

2 } On the count of one, find yourself in your Safe Place. Feel the beauty, love, blessed solitude, or enchantment of this place. Invite your Higher Self to join you. Sit with your legs crossed, facing each other.

3 } Together at the same time, you and your Higher Self slowly bend forward, toward each other, and touch foreheads. Close your mental eyes, and see and feel your Higher Self downloading into the center of your brain (more specifically the hypothalamus) a tiny sphere of light no bigger than a pea. Sit back up with your mental eyes still closed and sense the tiny sphere of light pulsating within the hypothalamus. This gentle sensation should not be uncomfortable, but if it is, ask your Higher Self to lower the frequency.

4 } After a time, see and feel—really *feel*—the sphere of light moving to the right side of your brain, where it will once again pulsate. After a time, see it moving to the left side of your brain, where it continues pulsating. The sphere then moves to the front of your brain and pulsates, and then after a while to the back of your brain, where it pulsates again.

5 } Now, see and feel the sphere moving from the left to the right hemisphere of your brain, and from the right to the left, back and forth. Then, see and feel the sphere moving back and forth from the front of your brain to the back.

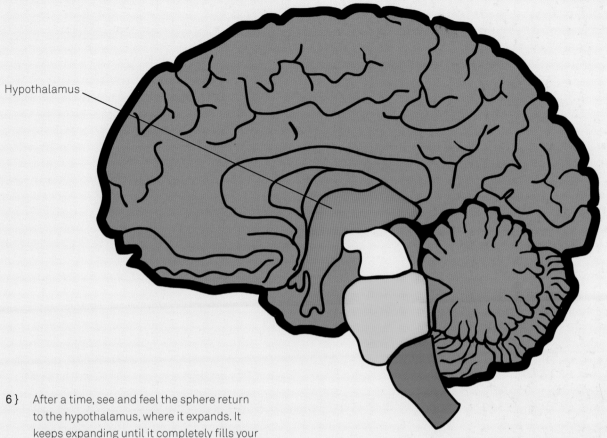

Hypothalamus

6 } After a time, see and feel the sphere return
to the hypothalamus, where it expands. It
keeps expanding until it completely fills your
entire brain.

7 } When your brain is filled with light, the pulsating stops and a faint humming sound begins.
Sit with the sound for a minute or two. After a
couple of minutes, the light and sound will dissipate and all will return to normal.

8 } Count mentally from one to five. On the count
of five, open your physical eyes and return.

We recommend lying down for a little while after completing this meditation, before you
return to your usual activities. Start out doing the meditation once per day for two weeks.
Thereafter, do it on a regular basis, perhaps once a week.

REDUCE THE SYMPTOMS OF ADHD

According to the Centers for Disease Control, five million children in the United States had been diagnosed with attention deficit hyperactivity disorder (ADHD) by 2006. An eight-week study, reported in the *Journal of Attention Disorders* in 2007, found that meditation reduced ADHD symptoms in 78 percent of those who participated in the study. Meditation, explains Dr. David Rabiner, director of undergraduate studies in the Department of Psychology and Neuroscience at Duke University, "can be thought of as an 'attention training' program."

The following active meditation is quick, easy, and effective—and kids enjoy doing it. It also helps adults improve their concentration, focus, and memory.

1 } Stand with your feet together, arms at your sides. Take a few slow, deep breaths to begin calming and centering yourself.

2 } Bring your hands up to your chest and press your palms together as if you were praying, with your thumbs resting against your breastbone. Choose a focal point and train your eyes on it.

3 } Inhale as you bend your knees and squat down, until you are in a position similar to sitting in a straight-backed chair. Keep your back straight. Your thighs should be at a 90-degree angle to your calves and your back. Stay in this position for a few moments.

4 } Exhale as you slowly come up to a standing position again.

5 } Repeat. Keep your eyes on the focal point you've chosen.

6 } Pay attention to your movements and your breath as you continue squatting and standing, in a slow, rhythmic manner.

7 } If your mind starts to wander or thoughts arise into your consciousness, simply let them go and return your attention to your breath and movements.

Perform this practice three times a day—in the morning, midday, and evening—for at least five minutes each time.

STRENGTHEN THE LEFT BRAIN-RIGHT BRAIN CONNECTION

A study of Buddhist monks, published in the *New York Times* in 2005, used magnetic resonance imaging (MRI) to view the effects of meditation on the participants' brains. The brain scans showed that as a result of meditation, the left prefrontal cortex (the site of joy) predominated over the right prefrontal cortex (the site of anxiety) in the monks.

The left side of your brain controls the right side of your body, for the most part, and the right side of the brain controls the left side of your body. The left brain is associated with rational thinking, analysis, and speech; the right brain, with intuition, imagination, and creativity. The following meditation helps balance the brain's two hemispheres and improve your mental functioning at all levels.

~~~~~~

1 } Stand with your feet about shoulder-width apart, knees slightly bent, hands at your sides. Take a few slow, deep breaths to relax and center yourself. Close your eyes if you like, but leave them open if necessary to maintain your balance.

2 } Shift your weight to your left foot and stand that way for a few moments. Slowly shift your weight to your right foot and stand that way for a few moments. You may notice you feel more comfortable or secure when your weight is on one foot or the other.

3 } Keep your mind focused on your body's movements. Continue slowly shifting your weight back and forth, from one foot to the other.

4 } Allow the rhythm of this gentle rocking motion to relax you further, bringing your mind and body into balance.

5 } If unwanted thoughts intrude into your awareness, simply let them go and return your attention to your movements.

6 } Continue this practice for as long as you like.

7 } When you feel ready, stop moving and, if your eyes are closed, open them.

Perform this meditation as often as you like, preferably for at least five minutes at a time.

RECOVER LOST MEMORIES AND EMOTIONS

Some memories are lost temporarily because you've suppressed them—the intensity of what you felt during past events was much too difficult to deal with at the time. Although the memories, along with the intensely charged emotions linked to them, are beyond your conscious awareness, they have not been erased. The traumatic energies of the event(s) will always remain deep within you, until you decide to bring them to the surface and heal them. If you leave them to fester, they will figuratively and literally "eat you" from the inside. If you allow them to surface (when you are ready) and choose to heal them, you can free yourself of the emotions along with the haunting memories, and retrieve the lost power and energy imprisoned within these memories.

Before beginning the following meditation, we recommend acquiring a smoky quartz crystal sphere, no less than 1 inch (5 cm) in diameter but no greater than 6 inches (12 cm) in diameter. Cleanse the crystal before meditation following the instructions on page 44 and after meditation following the instructions on page 45. When doing this meditation, hold the sphere comfortably on your lap. (Even without the benefit of the crystal, the meditation will work.)

1 } Sit or lie comfortably, with your eyes closed. Hold the smoky quartz crystal sphere on your lap. Take a deep breath and exhale. Do this two more times. Relax using whichever method you prefer.

2 } After you are relaxed, mentally count down from seven to one, relaxing more deeply with each count. On the count of one, find yourself in your Safe Place. Feel the beauty, love, blessed solitude, or enchantment of this place. Invite your Higher Self to join you. Sit together. Talk of your desire to retrieve a lost memory along with its emotion(s).

3 } Ask for the memory you are now ready to feel and release to surface. Your Higher Self would never bring anything up that you are not ready to handle, but it is good for you to say this anyway, to hear yourself acknowledge and intend it.

4 } Give the smoky quartz crystal sphere to your Higher Self. See or sense your Higher Self taking the sphere and placing it against its forehead, in the area of the third eye. After a short time, your Higher Self will return the sphere to you.

5 } Mentally place the sphere to your forehead. Feel the lost memories and emotions gently entering your brain. If you do not have a crystal sphere, sit facing your Higher Self. Together at the same time, you and your Higher Self slowly lean toward each other until you touch foreheads. Sit this way for a few moments as you feel your Higher Self downloading into your brain the lost memories and emotions.

6 } When all is completed, sit up straight again. You may sense a flowing sensation or a welling up of certain emotions. You may notice certain memories surfacing. Or, you may experience nothing at all. Whatever you experience—or not—know that in time memories will surface. You may experience deep emotions arising as well, ready to be healed.

7 } When you feel ready to exit the meditation, thank your Higher Self, close your mental eyes, and mentally count from one to five. On the count of five, open your physical eyes and return.

In time, memories and deeper emotions will surface, as you've requested. They may arise during your dreams. Remember, *you are healing, not being invaded.* Don't fight them or push them back down. If they come at an inconvenient time, ask your Higher Self to lift them from you and bring them back later when you can work with them. If you do this, you can release the emotions instead of having them surface on their own.

Hold the smoky quartz sphere while processing through the emotions. The crystal, and your Higher Self, will gradually and gently bring up the memories and emotions at a pace that's comfortable for you, and gradually help them dissolve. You need to reexperience these memories and feel these emotions, but you don't need to martyr yourself. You can now be released of barriers to success, happiness, and infinite possibilities. You can be free.

EXERCISE YOUR BRAIN TO IMPROVE CONCENTRATION AND FOCUS

Numerous studies in recent years have shown that meditation can increase concentration and focus. In May 2010, Harvard meditation expert Dr. Daniel Brown provided meditation training to sixty-six Massachusetts superior court judges. Brown says his objective was to help the judges concentrate without distraction, to be fully present in the courtroom, and to perform their duties with clearer minds.

The following meditation exercises the brain to improve your concentration and focus.

~~~~~~

1 } Sit or lie comfortably, with your eyes closed. Take a deep breath and exhale. Do this two more times. Relax using whichever method you prefer.

2 } After you are relaxed, mentally count down from seven to one, relaxing more deeply with each count. On the count of one, imagine yourself sitting in a comfortable chair in a darkened room.

3 } Imagine a three-dimensional sphere of white light, about the size of a bowling ball, approximately 7 to 8 feet (2 to 2.5 m) away from you. Imagine the sphere becoming bigger, then smaller. Keep alternating between bigger and smaller, smaller and bigger. Start slow, then gradually increase the speed. Keep this going until the shifting becomes so fast that it looks like the sphere is vibrating. After about a minute of this, stop and hold the sphere stationary in front of you.

4 } Now, imagine the sphere moving from right to left. Keep alternating the movement from right to left, left to right. Start slowly, and then gradually increase speed. Keep this going until the alternating becomes so fast that it looks like a flat, horizontal white line. After about a minute of this, stop and hold the sphere stationary in front of you. If this seems difficult at any stage, don't force it. Just do what you can do. It will improve with practice.

5 } Now, imagine the sphere moving from front to back. Keep alternating the movement from front to back, back to front. Start slowly, and then gradually increase speed. Keep this going until the alternating becomes so fast that the sphere looks like it's pulsating. After about a minute of this, stop and hold the sphere stationary in front of you.

6 } Now, imagine the sphere moving up and down. Keep alternating the movement up and down, down and up. Start slowly, and then gradually increase speed. Keep this going until the alternating becomes so fast that it looks like a flat vertical white line. After about a minute of this, stop and hold the sphere stationary in front of you.

7 } Now, imagine the sphere changing from white to red, then red to orange, orange to yellow, yellow to green, green to blue, blue to indigo, indigo to violet, and finally from violet back to white. Keep alternating the colors from white through red, orange, yellow, green, blue, indigo, violet, and back to white again. Do this for about a minute. When you're done, hold the white sphere in your awareness for a couple of seconds, and then see it fade away.

8 } Close your mental eyes and sit quietly for about a minute. When you're ready, mentally count from one to five. On the count of five, open your physical eyes and return.

Do this meditation for a few minutes each day. You'll soon notice the changes in your mental functioning.

Concentration is key to performance excellence—whether you're on the playing field or in the boardroom—and meditation is one of the best ways to improve your concentration. Meditators' brain waves, when measured by an EEG, rank higher on the Brain Integration Scale (BIS) than those of non-meditators. A study presented at the 2007 Conference of the American Psychological Association showed that thirty-three Norwegian gold medalists scored higher on the BIS than comparable athletes who didn't finish in the top ten.

MEDITATIONS TO
ENHANCE SUCCESS
AND PERFORMANCE

IMPROVE YOUR ATHLETIC ABILITY

"Training is about strengthening the mind-body connection," explains Kirsten Peterson, sports psychologist for the U.S. Olympic Committee. "Athletes need to train their minds with the same discipline that they train their bodies."

Many world-class athletes meditate, including Kobe Bryant, Michael Jordan, and Tiger Woods. Phil Jackson, head coach of the Los Angeles Lakers, meditates regularly and has encouraged members of his team to follow suit. The following meditation helps you improve your game by training your mind.

1 } Sit quietly in a comfortable place and close your eyes. Take a deep breath and exhale. Repeat two more times.

2 } Imagine yourself getting ready to play your favorite sport. See or sense yourself stepping up to the plate, walking out onto the tennis court, or taking your position on the tee.

3 } Feel yourself go through all the motions you normally engage in when you play your sport—but do it very slowly, paying careful attention to each movement. If you're playing tennis, for instance, watch the ball come over the net toward you at a much-reduced speed. Feel your body move toward it with agility and strength. Sense yourself swinging the racquet and smacking the ball, sending it flying back to your opponent's side of the court.

4 } See or sense yourself hit the ball again and again, scoring point after point, getting better and better—you never miss a shot. Bring all your senses into the experience. Make the scenario as vivid as possible. Feel your body and mind working together in complete harmony. Notice how calm, centered, and confident you are.

5 } Experience the joy of playing your sport—have fun.

6 } Play the game in your mind for as long as you like.

7 } When you feel ready, open your eyes.

Do this meditation as often as you like, for at least ten minutes at a time. Make it part of your regular training routine. The more you practice, the better you'll get.

PURSUE YOUR GOALS ONE STEP AT A TIME

An eight-week study conducted at the University of Pennsylvania in 2007 determined that meditation improved participants' ability to prioritize and manage their tasks and goals. As Richard J. Davidson, PhD, a researcher and neuroscientist at the University of Wisconsin who has been studying meditation's effects for two decades, explains, "Meditation can help you train your mind in the same way exercise can train your body."

This waking meditation draws upon the saying "A journey of a thousand miles begins with a single step" (attributed both to Taoist sage Lao Tsu and to Confucius). Use it to help you reach your goals.

~~~~~

1 } Take a walk to a destination you have pre-determined. Ideally, your destination should be one you are confident of reaching, but the walk should offer a few challenges (hills, for instance).

2 } Begin walking at a comfortable pace. Hold your goal or objective in your mind as you walk. Pay attention to each step you take. Feel the path beneath your feet. Sense the sun on your shoulders, the breeze on your face. Notice your body's motions, how your muscles work together to take you where you want to go. With each step, see or sense yourself moving closer to your goal.

3 } As you approach hills or other places along your walk that challenge you, equate them with challenges you face in pursuing your goal. You know you can master these challenges, just as you know without a doubt that you can walk to the top of the hills. Each time you crest a hill (or other challenge), feel a growing sense of strength and confidence.

4 } Release any uncertainty or anxiety about achieving your goal. Just as you are confident you will be able to reach your destination on this walk, know that you will be able to reach the life goal you've set for yourself.

5 } Don't rush or push yourself too hard. As you continue steadily putting one foot in front of the other, know that you can reach your goal in life by taking it one step at a time. Stay present as you walk. Even though you are headed toward a specific destination, enjoy the sights, sounds, smells, and other experiences along the way.

6 } Continue walking until you reach your destination. When you arrive at your journey's end, acknowledge your success in achieving this aim. Feel a sense of accomplishment and pleasure at having reached your destination.

7 } Connect your present feeling of accomplishment with what it will feel like when you achieve the life goal you've set for yourself.

Repeat this waking meditation whenever you wish to reinforce your determination or confidence.

THE BEST MEDITATIONS ON THE PLANET

RELEASE PERFORMANCE ANXIETY

Does your heart beat faster, your hands sweat, your mouth go dry, or your stomach tie itself in knots when you're in the spotlight? If so, you're not alone. Approximately 75 percent of us experience some type of performance anxiety. Even accomplished professionals often suffer from stage fright. An eight-week study of musicians, published in *Psychology of Music* in 2008, found that meditation improved participants' performance anxiety as well as their performance quality.

Whether you have stage fright, interview anxiety, first date jitters, or any other type of performance anxiety, the following meditation will help you feel grounded, protected, and confident.

~~~~~~

1 } Sit quietly in a place where you feel comfortable and close your eyes.

2 } Imagine a shaft of light, like a laser beam, descending from above you. Sense it enter the crown of your head and travel down through the center of your body.

3 } Feel the light move through each chakra and then exit your tailbone region (this experience may give you quite a rush). Imagine the shaft of light continuing its descent, all the way down to the very center of the Earth. See or sense the beam grounding you as it anchors you to the Earth.

4 } Now, imagine a sphere of luminescent light forming around you, like a cocoon. This sphere shields you and provides a sense of security.

5 } From your place within the sphere, ask your Higher Self to remove the anxiety you are experiencing.

6 } Feel the sphere drawing the anxiety and tension out of you and away from you.

7 } Remain in the meditation for as long as you like. When you feel ready, open your eyes.

Freed of the anxiety and tension, you can now enjoy the performance, the date, the interview. Periodically, notice that the shaft of light is still anchoring you and the luminescent sphere is still shielding you.

TRANSFORM INADEQUACY INTO EXCELLENCE

Feelings of inadequacy often stand in the way of our success. Discouraging words, as researchers at North Carolina State University discovered, can also adversely affect our ability to perform. In a study of 153 people age sixty to eighty-two, published in *Experimental Aging Research* in 2009, subjects performed more poorly on memory tests when primed with words such as *confused, feeble*, and *senile* than they did when primed with positive words such as *accomplished, dignified*, and *distinguished*. Lead researcher Dr. Thomas Hess told BBC News, "It may be that if people can suppress these negative thoughts [then] they will do much better, and that a positive attitude can promote effective functioning."

The following meditation uses words to let you replace negative thinking patterns with positive ones, in order to improve your performance in any area of life.

~~~~~~

1 } Sit or lie comfortably, with your eyes closed. Take a deep breath and exhale. Do this two more times. Relax using whichever method you prefer.

2 } Bring to mind a word that stirs up a feeling of inadequacy for you, such as *cowardice*. Now think of a word that expresses the opposite, such as *courage*.

3 } As you inhale, think the word *courage* and imagine you are actually taking courage into yourself. Feel yourself becoming more courageous as the word resonates in your mind and fills your body. As you exhale, think the word *cowardice* and imagine you are eliminating cowardice from yourself. Feel the unwanted condition diminishing as you release it with your breath.

4 } Think of another word that brings up a feeling of inadequacy for you, such as *clumsiness*. Now think of a word that expresses the opposite, such as *grace*. As you inhale, think the word *grace* and imagine you are actually taking grace into your body. Feel yourself becoming more graceful as the word resonates in your mind and fills your body. As you exhale, think the word *clumsiness* and imagine you are eliminating clumsiness from yourself.

5 } Feel the unwanted condition diminishing as you release it with your breath.

6 } Continue in this manner, choosing up to ten words that represent negative qualities you wish to transform into positive ones. Inhale the positive quality, and exhale the negative one.

7 } When you've finished working through your list and feel ready, open your eyes.

MEDITATE TO GET "IN THE ZONE"

Elevating your athletic performance, as in all areas of life, requires getting out of your own way. You've probably heard the term "in the zone." Physicists call it "frictionless flow," a state in which you encounter no resistance to anything you do. When you are in the zone, you:

- stay focused without strain;
- are "in the moment," free of mental noise;
- experience mind-body harmony and the rhythm of the game;
- feel the exhilaration of the game without being overwhelmed by it.

Many top-level athletes use meditation, relaxation and breathing exercises, and visualization to help them get in the zone. These practices reduce the mental chatter that causes distraction and undermines success. If you're like most people, you talk to yourself at a rate of several hundred words per minute. Replacing that chatter with images can improve your athletic performance, too. Jeff Simons, a sports psychologist at California State University, recommends that athletes "imagine competing, getting in their own groove, feeling it, tasting it, [remembering] that feeling of flow."

Remember a time when playing sports was fun? Remember playing without the pressure to "win, win, win"? If you lost, you were disappointed, but you got back up, brushed yourself off, and worked to improve your game so you'd play better next time. Once you've experienced being in the zone, you can duplicate it. The following meditation helps you recapture that enjoyable experience of athletic nirvana.

~~~~~~

1 } Sit or lie comfortably, with your eyes closed. Take a deep breath and exhale. Do this two more times. Relax using whichever method you prefer. After you are relaxed, mentally count down from seven to one, relaxing more deeply with each count.

2 } On the count of one, find yourself in your Safe Place. Feel the beauty, love, blessed solitude, or enchantment of this place.

3 } Invite your Higher Self to join you. Ask your Higher Self to help you bring back the memory, along with the experience, of being "in the zone."

(continued on page 128)

4 } Now, close your mental eyes, and be still. Let memories flow. Maybe when you were a child or an adolescent you experienced the zone while playing a game or some other activity. Maybe you recall a time as an adult when everything just seemed to flow and whatever you did "clicked."

5 } If you remember such an experience, play it over and over in your mind. Feel what it was like. Be in that zone once again. After a few minutes of remembering, open your mental eyes.

6 } Your Higher Self hands you a small object. This object holds the resonance of this experience. Whenever you think of the object, you will trigger the experience of being in the zone—not just the memory of the event, but the actual experience.

7 } Thank your Higher Self.

8 } Close your mental eyes and count mentally from one to five. On the count of five, open your physical eyes and return.

If you could not remember such an experience, don't worry—eventually you will recall one, or perhaps experience one for the first time. Your intention is everything. Before you begin any athletic activity or game, take a minute or two and close your eyes and imagine the object. Feel the shift take place. If you wish, you can choose a small, physical object to serve as your token or touchstone. Carry the object in your pocket when you play your sport. Whenever you touch your token, it will help trigger the zone experience. The more you practice this meditation, the easier it will be for you to enter the zone and stay there.

CHOOSE POSITIVE OUTCOMES FOR THE FUTURE

The future may be a crapshoot, but you can always load the dice. Although you never know what lies ahead, you can exercise the power of choice to ensure a more favorable outcome. Nothing is etched in stone until you chisel it there. No medical diagnosis is a death sentence until you sign it. And no outcome is certain until you choose it.

The Ohio Longitudinal Study of Aging and Retirement, which involved 1,157 people age fifty-plus over a twenty-year period, found that individuals with positive attitudes lived nearly eight years longer on average than their pessimistic counterparts. A 2008–2009 University of Missouri study of 327 job seekers determined that people who maintained optimistic attitudes while searching for employment were more likely to receive job offers than those with less positive attitudes.

When you are faced with a future event that is uncertain and perhaps frightening (a medical procedure, an exam, an important meeting or interview, a legal decision), the following meditation increases your chance of a favorable outcome by helping you release anxiety and let go of your attachment to a specific result.

~~~~~~

1 } Before doing the meditation, think for a moment about the worst possible outcome the event could have. Don't worry—you aren't increasing that possibility by considering it. You'll actually give your fear more power by repressing or ignoring it. Now, think of the best possible outcome. When you are ready, proceed with the meditation.

2 } Sit or lie comfortably, with your eyes closed. Take a deep breath and exhale. Do this two more times. Relax using whichever method you prefer. After you are relaxed, mentally count down from seven to one, relaxing more deeply with each count.

3 } On the count of one, find yourself in your Safe Place. Feel the beauty, love, blessed solitude, or enchantment of this place.

4 } Invite your Higher Self to join you. Sit together. Talk of this future event. Feel the emotions— worry? anxiety? doubt?—that come up as you talk about it. When you are finished, your Higher Self draws a mist or fog into your Safe Place. It becomes so thick you can't see anything around you. Your Higher Self gently takes you by the hand and guides you through the mist/fog to the other side. On the other side you find yourself standing in a candlelit room before two doors. Behind one door is the worst possible outcome; behind the other door is the best. Your Higher Self points to the door that leads to the worst possible outcome. Enter it.

(continued on page 130)

5 } Once inside, watch the worst possible outcome play out. If the future event is a job interview, observe yourself being rejected. If the event is a medical test, observe the doctor informing you of the finding you fear. If it is an important meeting, see it becoming a disaster. Notice yourself in the event, but don't *be* that person. Just observe it from a "third person" perspective. It is important, however, that you feel what you would feel, here. Don't hold back. Notice how much energy you are expending to this possible outcome. Take a moment to draw back into yourself this energy that you have been losing. Feel a wonderful rush of energy and vitality returning to you. When you are finished, exit the scene and find yourself standing once again at that door. With your mind, dissolve the door and everything behind it. Watch it fade away until it is totally gone.

6 } Now enter the door that leads to the best possible outcome. Once inside, experience the best possible outcome. Experience everything as if you are really living it. Experience yourself getting the job. Experience the doctor informing you that you are in perfect health. Experience the important meeting as a remarkable success. Feel what you would feel—joy, relief, excitement, celebration. Don't hold back. Feel the energy and vitality you retrieved earlier. Allow this positive energy to flow into this space, filling it with your joy and excitement.

7 } When you are finished, exit the scene and find yourself standing once again at that door. With your mind, illuminate the door and the best possible outcome. Watch it become luminescent and vibrant.

8 } Say to yourself, "This or better." Thank your Higher Self, then close your mental eyes and mentally count from one to five. On the count of five, open your physical eyes and return.

Do this meditation whenever you feel anxious or doubtful about a future situation or event.

TURN OFF OTHER PEOPLE'S JUDGMENTS

Our success—or lack of it—may be linked to the judgments other people made about us when we were too young to assess those judgments. If people we respect criticize us, put us down, or are unsupportive of us, their influence may limit what we accomplish in life. If they encourage us, however, we're more likely to succeed. According to a study released by the Cooperative Institutional Research Program at UCLA in 2007, nearly half of first-generation college students said parental encouragement was the main reason they went on to pursue higher education. Another study of black students, published in the *Canadian Journal of Education* in 2007, found that students who received support and encouragement from their parents achieved academic success, despite adversity in other areas of life.

The following meditation helps you detach from the limitations of someone else's judgment.

1 } Sit or lie comfortably, with your eyes closed. Relax using whichever method you prefer. After you are somewhat relaxed mentally, count down from seven to one, relaxing more deeply with each count. When you are ready, imagine you are sitting in a comfortable chair, across the room from a television set.

2 } Pick up the remote control and turn on the TV. On the screen you see a person who discouraged, criticized, or belittled you in the past. Observe this person as he or she says negative things about you. Notice that he/she keeps saying the same things over and over, like a rerun you've seen many times before.

3 } Simply observe the person on the TV screen. Don't let your mind form other images or scenarios that "flesh out" the subject of his/her commentary. You realize this person can do nothing to harm you—he or she is merely a two-dimensional image on the television. He/she has no power over you. You feel no reaction to the person's incessant monologue. You understand that he/she is expressing his/her opinions, nothing more. He/she could be talking about anyone—you remain completely detached.

4 } Use the remote control to turn the volume down until you can only see the person's lips moving soundlessly.

5 } When you grow tired of observing this person, pick up the remote control and press the OFF button.

6 } When the screen goes blank, mentally count from one to five.

7 } Open your eyes on the count of five.

When you feel you've freed yourself from the negative opinions of one person, do the same meditation with someone else who also disparaged you.

IMPROVE FOCUS, PERSISTENCE, AND FOLLOW-THROUGH

A 2007 study conducted at the University of Pennsylvania examined students over an eight-week period to determine how meditation might impact their cognitive ability. At the end of the study, participants took computerized tests. The students who meditated demonstrated greater focus and accuracy and the ability to manage tasks and prioritize goals better than the control group.

Because meditation shifts your focus to the here and now, it can help you stick with a task and see it through to completion. This has positive implications for job satisfaction and performance—whether you're doing repetitious, routine tasks or making executive decisions—and for producing outcomes as well. The following meditation uses a Zen technique of emphasizing the process instead of the goal. By keeping your attention on the task at hand, the meditation strengthens your focus, patience, and persistence.

~~~~~~

1 } Acquire a piece of rope, cord, string, or lacing at least 2 feet (61 cm) in length. Sit in a quiet place where you feel comfortable. Near one end of the rope, tie a loose knot. Focus your attention completely on the process of tying the knot. When you've finished, tie another loose knot a few inches from the first knot. Then tie another.

2 } Work slowly and methodically, keeping your attention on your task.

3 } If your mind starts to wander or you catch yourself becoming bored, take a deep breath and exhale. Then bring your attention back to the details of your task.

4 } Appreciate the dexterity with which your fingers function. Notice the numerous movements you must make to create each knot.

5 } Continue the process until you've tied as many knots as you can in the piece of rope.

6 } Now, reverse the process and begin untying the knots one at a time.

7 } Work slowly and methodically, keeping your attention on what you're doing.

8 } When you've untied all the knots, repeat the process.

Continue in this manner for as long as you like, but do at least two repetitions (tie and untie all the knots twice). The practice will also help ground you in the moment and increase your attention span.

If you prefer, you can substitute another task that emphasizes the process instead of the outcome. For example, collect small stones and pile them one by one into a mound, then move them to form another mound. Rake sand on a beach, then let the waves wash away the marks; use a cup to transfer water from one container to another and back again. Or, create a Zen sand painting. The purpose is to strengthen your ability to focus your attention by learning to stay in the moment, rather than thinking about the future.

CLIMB THE STAIRWAY TO SUCCESS

As scientific research upholds the benefits of meditation, corporations of all kinds are instituting meditation programs for their employees. Many of the corporate world's most accomplished individuals credit meditation with being a significant component in their success. For example, Medtronic's former CEO, Bill George, says, "Out of anything, [meditation] has had the greatest impact on my career." Michael Stephen, former chairman of Aetna International, says meditation helped him become a more effective leader.

The following meditation lets you focus on your goals and take the steps necessary to accomplish your objectives.

~~~~~

1 } Sit or lie comfortably, with your eyes closed. Take a deep breath and exhale. Do this two more times. Relax using whichever method you prefer. Imagine you are standing at the foot of a stairway. This stairway leads to the success you seek in your professional or personal life. At the top of the stairs is the goal you intend to achieve—graduating from college, getting a job, losing weight, winning a contest, or whatever you desire.

2 } Mentally associate each step of the stairway with a step on the way to your goal. For example, if your goal is to graduate from college, each step might represent a course or a semester. If your goal is to lose weight, each step could stand for 2 or 10 pounds (1 or 5 kg). The number of steps is up to you.

3 } When you are ready, see or sense yourself ascending to the first step. As you stand on the step, imagine it lighting up and shining with a beautiful golden glow. Pause for a few moments and feel the sense of achievement and satisfaction at having reached this step. Move to the second step. Again, when you put your weight on the step it glows with golden light. Feel great pride of accomplishment as you stand on this illuminated step. Ascend to the third step. Notice how it glows and how happy you feel at having reached this step in your journey. Continue climbing the stairs, one step at a time.

4 } Allow yourself to pause briefly on each step to enjoy your growing sense of self-esteem and confidence. Give yourself as much time as you need to climb the stairway. There's no rush to reach the top within a set amount of time. What's important is to feel the joy of accomplishment with each step you take.

5 } When you arrive at the top of the stairway, congratulate yourself on having accomplished your goal. Look down at all the illuminated steps you've mounted and know that you have earned your position at the top of the stairway.

6 } Shout, pat yourself on the back, clap your hands, or react in any way you choose to express your pleasure. Spend as long as you like experiencing joy, pride, satisfaction, optimism—or whatever you feel at having made it to the top. When you're ready, open your eyes.

Do this meditation whenever you feel a need to bolster your self-confidence, especially when faced with challenges or obstacles that intimidate you and make you question your ability to accomplish your goal. If you like, you may do this as a waking meditation. Find a stairway you can physically climb and connect each step with a step in your process. As you physically mount the stairs, envision yourself working your way toward your goal, one step at a time.

USE YOUR CELL PHONE TO IMPROVE YOUR PERFORMANCE

Modern brain wave technology, along with advanced audio delivery systems such as iPods, cell phones, and various popular audio systems, are making groundbreaking advances in the experience of altered states of consciousness. Using what's called "binaural brain wave entrainment," researchers and audio technicians are producing amazing results in these areas:

- Problem solving
- Improved sleep
- Enhanced states of deep relaxation
- Concentration and alertness
- Improvement in moods and attitudes
- Increased energy and stamina
- Experiences of bliss and states of well-being

Different states of awareness are associated with different brain wave frequencies. During your everyday waking state of beta consciousness, for example, your brain wave frequencies are about 13 to 30 cycles per second (cps). During meditation, they decrease to about 8 to 13 cps, the alpha level of consciousness. By using binaural brain wave entrainment, these frequencies can be easily induced. A growing number of studies report changes in consciousness associated with binaural entrainment.

According to University of Virginia researcher Justine E. Owens, PhD, and F. Holmes Atwater, research director of the Monroe Institute, "The subjective effect of listening to binaural beats may be relaxing or stimulating, depending on the frequency of the binaural-beat stimulation." Binaural beats in the delta (1 to 4 Hz) and theta (4 to 8 Hz) ranges have been associated with relaxed, meditative, and creative states, and can aid sleep, explains Canadian psychologist and author Chok C. Hiew, PhD. Research done in 1990 by Dale S. Foster, PhD, psychologist at the Memphis Integral Neurofeedback Institute, showed that binaural beats in the alpha frequencies increased alpha brain waves. Binaural beats in the beta frequencies improved memory, according to studies by La Mesa, California, clinical psychologist Richard Cauley Kennerly, PhD, in 1994.

Martin uses a program called "Brain Wave – 20 Binaural Programs" (available for iPod/iPhone through Banzai Labs, www.brainwaveapps.com). A high school baseball umpire and soccer referee, Martin spends ten to fifteen minutes before each game listening on his iPhone to a specific program that helps him get energetically charged and mentally focused. After the game, he listens to another program to achieve deep, stress-free relaxation. He swears by the programs' efficacy.

You'll find many brain wave entrainment programs on the market. Some are good, some less so. Do your homework and select the one that seems right for you.

Stress can adversely impact our relationships with the people in our lives, so it's no surprise that meditation, by reducing stress and anxiety, can help us get along better with loved ones, coworkers, and friends. A study of employees in both large and small companies, published in the journal *Anxiety, Stress, & Coping*, found that meditation improved employees' relationships at home as well as on the job.

MEDITATIONS TO IMPROVE RELATIONSHIPS

THE BEST MEDITATIONS ON THE PLANET

HONOR THE DIVINE WITHIN EVERYONE

Namaste (pronounced nah-mah-STAY) is a Sanskrit word that literally means "I bow to you with reverence." It can also be translated as "I honor the Spirit (or the Divine) within you" or "The light within me salutes the light within you." Sometimes spoken as a salutation, the word *namaste* acknowledges that we are more than what we appear to be on the outside, and that all of us are sparks of light materialized from a Higher Source. This meditation helps you look beyond a person's behavior to see his or her inner goodness.

~~~~~~

1 } Sit in a place where you feel comfortable and close your eyes. Relax using whichever method you prefer. Mentally call the name of a person with whom you are experiencing a challenge.

2 } See or sense that person's presence before you. Allow yourself to experience whatever feelings you have toward this person, particularly if those feelings are unpleasant or upsetting to you. Now, say the word *namaste*, followed by the person's name. You may speak the word aloud or simply say it mentally. See or sense the other person receiving your greeting. You may perceive this as a light glowing in the area around his or her heart.

3 } Say *namaste* again. Acknowledge that the person before you is more than a body, more than his/her words, more than his/her actions.

4 } Say *namaste* again, and feel a warm, gentle glow in the region of your own heart.

5 } Say *namaste* again, and see or sense a connection between your heart and the other person's. You may experience a slight tingling or warmth in your chest.

6 } Repeat the word *namaste* until your anger, sadness, or other emotions dissipate.

7 } When you feel ready, bow your head slightly to the other person and release him/her. Open your eyes.

You can perform a quick version of this meditation anytime, anyplace, whenever you feel annoyed, anxious, hurt, or displeased with someone. Close your eyes and think *namaste* to acknowledge the divine essence in the other person—and in yourself.

GAIN APPRECIATION FOR OTHERS THROUGH CULTIVATING LOVING-KINDNESS

Buddhist tradition teaches an ancient concept known as "loving-kindness," which involves compassion and appreciation for all living creatures. As the Dalai Lama explains, "My religion is kindness." Buddhists say that through cultivating the practice of loving-kindness, known as *Metta Bhavana*, we can dissolve the barriers between us that perpetuate fear and suffering in the world.

The loving-kindness meditation that follows helps you gain a greater appreciation of the people in your life so you can share their joy, rather than feeling jealous, competitive, or alienated. You can use this meditation to engender compassionate feelings and understanding toward the people closest to you (family, spouse, friends), someone you respect (a wise teacher, for instance), a neutral person or someone you don't know, or an "enemy" (someone with whom you experience difficulty or challenges).

~~~~~

1 } Sit quietly in a place where you feel comfortable and close your eyes. Take a deep breath and exhale. Do this two more times. Relax using whichever method you prefer. Focus on your breathing until your mind and body grow quiet.

2 } Begin contemplating the kindness and generosity other people have shown to you, beginning with your parents, who gave you your body. Consider the people who provided shelter and food for you, before you were capable of obtaining these for yourself. Think of those who educated you, who taught you the skills you needed to function in the world.

3 } Now contemplate all the people whose efforts contribute to your daily well-being: farmers who grow the food you eat, road crews who maintain the highways on which you drive, oil workers who provide fuel for your car, garbage haulers who collect your trash, doctors and nurses who care for you when you're sick, and so on. Consider how you rely on other people for virtually everything in your life that you usually take for granted: the books you read, the movies you enjoy, the clothing you wear, the music you listen to, the electricity in your home, and so on.

4 } Even though these people may not intend to perform a kindness for you when they do something, you benefit from their labors nonetheless, and therefore they are worthy of your gratitude. Focus on the benefits you receive, not on their motivations (which you can't possibly know anyway).

5 } Even people who test you offer you a service. They enable you to grow stronger and develop essential qualities such as patience, perseverance, and forgiveness that are necessary for your enlightenment. Acknowledge that you cannot separate yourself from others or exist without other people. We are all interconnected and interdependent upon one another.

6 } Make a commitment to cherish other people and appreciate innumerable ways in which they contribute to your well-being, whether or not you are aware of their contributions.

7 } Dedicate the positive energy raised during this meditation to maintaining the welfare of all beings. When you feel ready, slowly open your eyes.

Perform this meditation often, especially when you feel irritated, isolated, or fearful where other people are concerned. As you go about your day-to-day activities, keep in mind that everyone you meet is inherently important, that his or her happiness and well-being are important.

WIPE AWAY THE GRIME OF RESENTMENT

Holding on to the bitterness of resentment is like drinking poison and expecting someone else to die. According to an article published in October 2000 in the international medical journal *Cancer Nursing*, "Suppressed anger can be a precursor to the development of cancer, and also a factor in its progression after diagnosis." Even if resentment doesn't lead to disease, it can damage your relationships with other people and block your own happiness.

This meditation helps you cleanse resentment's obfuscating effects from your thinking, so you can see other people and your situation with clarity. You can also perform the meditation mentally with your eyes closed.

1 } Collect the equipment/materials needed to wash a window.

2 } Select a dirty window in your own home (or in another place where you feel safe and where you will not be disturbed for at least ten to fifteen minutes).

3 } Call to mind a person and/or relationship situation toward which you harbor unresolved anger and resentment.

4 } Stand before the window; feel your resentment well up in your chest, stomach, or another part of your body. Look at the window as if it were a portal through which to view a problem that is troubling you. See the dirt and grime on the window as representing your feelings of resentment. Notice how the grime on the glass interferes with your ability to see clearly your own situation, which lies just beyond the window.

5 } Begin washing the window. Spray cleanser on the glass and start wiping away the dust and dirt with your cleaning cloth. As you work, imagine you are wiping away the grime that inhibits your ability to accurately view a troubling relationship. Each swipe of your cleaning cloth enables you to view the situation with greater clarity.

6 } Keep your mind focused on your task. If unrelated thoughts pop into your consciousness, gently ease them aside for the time being. If any insights or emotions related to your situation emerge, take note of them.

7 } Continue washing the window, wiping away the grime of resentment that blocks your understanding, until you feel you can see the situation and the person(s) involved more clearly.

Repeat this practice as often as necessary, for as long as is comfortable for you.

SILENCE JUDGMENT TO REDUCE RELATIONSHIP STRESS

Disputes with the people we know often arise from the judgments we've made about them. When we point fingers and judge other people to be wrong, we experience frustration, disappointment, anger, anxiety, or other unpleasant emotions. We also set up an "us vs. them" situation. Our reactions generate stress and unhappiness in our relationships.

The following practice helps you become aware of the judgments you make every day. By paying attention to how you judge others, you can reduce the stress you experience when relating to other people and ease tensions with family members, partners, and coworkers.

~~~~~

1 } Notice each time you make a verbal or mental judgment about someone else. *That idiot pulled right out in front of me! That woman is so fat, how can she let herself get that way? He's stupid to believe that crazy idea.* And so on . . .

2 } Notice each time you use these words: should, must, ought to, got to, have to, need to.

3 } Just observe what you say and think. Each time you catch yourself judging or criticizing someone, simply acknowledge it by mentally saying *judgment*.

4 } Don't judge or blame yourself for having judgmental thoughts.

5 } In time, you'll discover that you aren't as quick to find fault with others. Your desire to change them lessens. You can observe the people in your life without criticizing them or judging them to be wrong.

6 } You'll also find that your own stress level diminishes, as does the tension between you and other people.

7 } Make this practice a part of your everyday life.

Continually monitor your moralistic evaluations and criticisms of other people.

RECLAIM YOUR SHADOW

In his book *Archetypes and the Collective Unconscious*, Swiss analyst Carl G. Jung wrote about the concept of projection, which means we see our own repressed attributes—especially those we dislike—mirrored in other people. Jung called this unconscious part of us the "Shadow." Projecting disowned traits and qualities can damage your relationships and drain your vitality. This meditation allows you to reclaim your Shadow and integrate it into your own personality.

~~~~~~

1 } Sit in a place where you feel comfortable and close your eyes. Take a deep breath and exhale. Do this two more times. Relax using whichever method you prefer. After you are somewhat relaxed mentally, count down from seven to one, relaxing more deeply with each number.

2 } On the count of one, sense that you are in your Safe Place. Feel the beauty, love, blessed solitude, or enchantment of this place. Invite your Higher Self to join you.

3 } While sitting beside your Higher Self, bring to mind a person you know—a life partner, family member, coworker, friend, and so on—and imagine him/her sitting or standing, facing you. Spend a few moments connecting with this person, until you feel his/her presence strongly.

4 } See or sense splotches of colored light attached to this person's body. These splotches are your projections, pieces of your Shadow. This emotional energy belongs to you, but you have cast it out and fixed it onto the other person, without realizing what you were doing.

5 } What color(s) are these patches of light? Where are they placed on the person's body? Focus your attention on one patch of color. Inhale slowly, and as you do, see or sense this patch pulling away from the other person's body as you draw the light into your own lungs. Feel the light being reabsorbed into your body, then exhale slowly.

6 } You may experience an emotion, a tingling sensation, a surge of vitality, or another feeling. You might also gain insights or awareness as you take back your projected energy.

7 } When you're ready, focus on another patch of colored light and repeat the process. Continue removing colored patches from the other person's body until you've reclaimed all your projected energy, or until you decide you've done enough for one session.

8 } Thank the other person for participating, and release him/her. Allow his/her image to slowly dissolve from your awareness.

9 } When you feel ready, open your eyes.

When you've finished removing your projections from one person, do the same thing with other people you know.

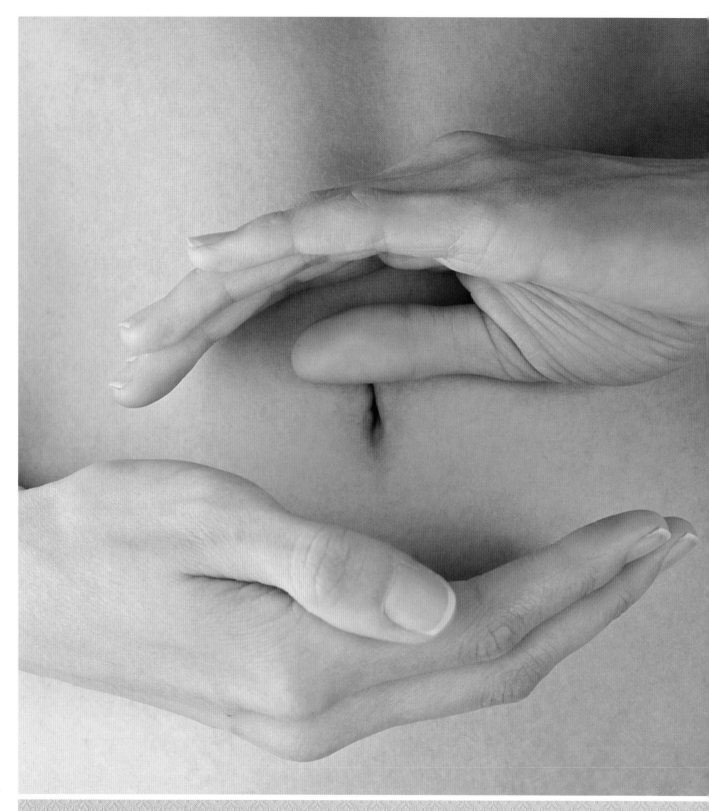

BUILD SEXUAL ENERGY

In her book *The Art of Sexual Ecstasy*, Margo Anand writes, "Meditation helps you bring heightened awareness to the body, heart, and mind and to tune these three aspects of your being into a harmony that allows higher, more intense levels of pleasurable experience."

Eastern medicine connects the sacral chakra, the body's energy center located about a hand's width below your belly button, with sexuality. When this chakra is blocked or otherwise imbalanced, various types of sexual dysfunction can result. The following meditation stimulates the flow of energy into the sacral chakra to increase sexual vitality.

~~~~~~

1 } Sit or lie comfortably with your eyes closed. Take a deep breath and exhale. Do this two more times. Relax using whichever method you prefer.

2 } Bring your attention to the root chakra, the energy center located at the base of your spine. Imagine a spark of fire glowing at this part of your body. Deepen your breathing, and as you do, sense this spark burning more brightly. See or sense your breath "fanning the flame" and causing the fire to grow higher.

3 } Feel the pleasing warmth generated by the fire. Sense its red-orange glow spreading through the lower part of your body. See or sense the fire swelling upward, into your sacral chakra. Feel the fire's pleasing warmth spreading into your lower abdomen.

4 } Feel this part of your body becoming energized and enlivened by the fire. Allow sensual feelings to emerge and gradually intensify. Don't try to suppress them.

5 } Rather than being localized in the genitals, these pleasurable feelings radiate through your hips and abdomen. You may experience them streaming into your thighs, your chest, or other parts of your body as well. If thoughts arise into your awareness, simply let them go and bring your attention back to the fire glowing within you. Stay with these feelings for as long as you like.

6 } When you're ready, sense the fire slowly diminishing, burning down until only a bed of hot coals remains at the base of your spine. Know that the next time you wish to raise this energy, all you have to do is mentally blow on the coals and ignite the fire.

7 } Open your eyes.

Do this meditation regularly, for at least ten to fifteen minutes at a time, to strengthen sexual response and enhance pleasure.

STRENGTHEN A RELATIONSHIP

In the law of synergy, the whole is greater than the sum of its parts. In the law of relationships, the relationship is greater than the sum of the people in it. When you look at a relationship from the perspective of mathematics, 1 + 1 = 3 (you, your partner, and the relationship). The love within the relationship is greater than the people involved, and even if difficulties or tensions exist, the relationship is still stronger than both individuals. Working through a difficult relationship isn't about "fixing the other person." It may require putting more trust in the relationship than in yourself or your partner. By focusing less on the components and more on the whole, the relationship may grow stronger over time and also strengthen both people involved. The following meditation can help.

~~~~~~~

1 } Sit or lie comfortably with your eyes closed. Take a deep breath and exhale. Do this two more times. Relax using whichever method you prefer. After you are relaxed, mentally count down from seven to one, relaxing more deeply with each count.

2 } On the count of one, find yourself in your Safe Place. Feel the beauty, love, blessed solitude, or enchantment of this place. Invite your Higher Self to join you. Sit together. Talk of your desire to strengthen a relationship. Now, invite the other person and his/her Higher Self (in meditation only, not physically) to join you.

3 } You and your partner stand several yards (meters) apart, facing each other. Ask your Higher Selves to stand beside you. Send from your hearts beams of white light. This light is the love you have for each other.

4 } Imagine the light from both your hearts touching in the middle of the space that separates you. At the point of contact, a tiny sphere forms. It grows bigger and bigger until it becomes a huge sphere of light 10 to 15 feet (3 to 5 m) in diameter. You and your Higher Self and your partner and his/her Higher Self enter the sphere at the same time.

5 } Inside the sphere do nothing but close your mental eyes and feel the power of love healing, nurturing, and above all raising your resonance to a higher, more loving level.

6 } Stay in this blissful place energetically for a couple of minutes (or longer if you wish). When you are ready, keep your mental eyes closed and mentally count from one to five.

7 } On the count of five, open your physical eyes and return.

Do this meditation whenever you feel the need to strengthen and reconnect with the synergy of the relationship. If you feel it's appropriate, you may ask your partner to join you in doing the meditation.

BECOME A BETTER RECEIVER

Many of us are wonderful givers, but lousy receivers. If a friend is in need, we give abundantly of ourselves and our resources. But we may find it difficult to receive or to accept what others offer us. A relationship, however, is a two-way street. Unless we can be givers as well as receivers, we can't fully engage with other people. If a pitcher does not have a catcher to throw to, how is he going to be a better pitcher? The same holds true in our relationships. If someone offers love, but no one is available to receive it, how is s/he going to become more loving? Our reluctance to receive may be rooted in these fears:

- Fear of obligation
- Fear of intimacy
- Fear of losing control
- Fear of abandonment, betrayal, humiliation, or rejection
- Fear of vulnerability
- And many other reasons

Receiving takes great courage and strength—the courage to let fear go and allow yourself to be vulnerable. Remember, also, that there's a difference between being a "receiver" and being a "taker." By letting someone give to you, you honor the giver and share his/her joy. Everyone gains, and no one loses.

~~~~~~

1 } Sit or lie comfortably, with your eyes closed. Take a deep breath and exhale. Do this two more times. Relax using whichever method you prefer. After you are relaxed, mentally count down from seven to one, relaxing more deeply with each count.

2 } On the count of one, find yourself in your Safe Place. Feel the beauty, love, blessed solitude, or enchantment of this place. Invite your Higher Self to join you. Talk of your desire to practice receiving.

3 } Now, both of you stand (in the meditation). Turn your back to your Higher Self. Your Higher Self will place its hands on your back.

4 } Very slowly drop backward while your Higher Self supports you. Lean all your weight against your Higher Self. Lean back further and further until you are completely reliant on your Higher Self's support. Experience your total vulnerability. Close your mental eyes and stay in this vulnerable position for a few minutes. Emotions may surface—let them.

5 } After a while, your Higher Self will gently bring you back to an upright position. Thank your Higher Self and embrace. Feel its love for you. Ask for help to further heal your resistances to receiving from others.

6 } Now, close your mental eyes and mentally count from one to five.

7 } On the count of five, open your physical eyes and return.

This meditation may seem difficult at first but don't give up. Be willing to receive its gift. During the next few days, emotions may surface. Don't push them down. Feel them and let them go. Do this meditation regularly to increase your receptivity. In addition, practice saying "yes" when people offer to give you something or do something for you.

END TIES THAT BIND

Letting a relationship go can be difficult. Whether the relationship is one from your past or a part of your current experience, moving beyond it may seem a daunting task. We hope that time will help us heal, and more often than not, it does. But sometimes, even time cannot break the ties that bind you to the relationship. The following meditation is designed to provide a smooth and highly effective means to let go, once and for all.

1 } Sit or lie comfortably, with your eyes closed. Take a deep breath and exhale. Do this two more times. Relax using whichever method you prefer. After you are relaxed, mentally count down from seven to one, relaxing more deeply with each count.

2 } On the count of one, find yourself in your Safe Place. Feel the beauty, love, blessed solitude, or enchantment of this place. Invite your Higher Self to join you.

3 } Now, find a long stick and with it draw a large circle on the ground. Call in the other person. He or she will appear within the circle. Insist that all ties and connections between the two of you be severed. The other person may object, but you remain firm. In time, he or she will agree.

4 } Now, sense a white cord extending from your navel to the navel of the other person. Feel a rush of energy flowing from the other person through the white cord and into you. Really feel it—it will be a powerful and elevating experience.

5 } When your energy has been returned to you, take the white cord and disconnect it from your navel. It is common to experience grief at this time. Feel it deeply—it needs to be felt.

6 } Now, lean into your Higher Self's arms. Your Higher Self will mend the hole in your stomach where the cord once was and will fill the space with love. Feel the love and the nurturing.

7 } Now, close your mental eyes and mentally count from one to five. On the count of five, open your physical eyes and return.

You may need to repeat this meditation in order to completely sever the ties between you and the other person. Do it as often as necessary until you feel free to move on.

FOCUS ON FORGIVENESS

According to C. Norman Shealy, MD, PhD, founder of the American Holistic Medical Association and President of Holos University, "Forgiveness produces miracles; lack of forgiveness inhibits miracles." Best-selling author Marianne Williamson explains in *A Return to Love*, "Forgiveness is a selective remembering—a conscious decision to focus on love and let the rest go."

So long as you concentrate on what's "wrong" in a relationship, you'll avoid seeing what's right. You'll also stay stuck in the unhappiness and resentment produced by your memories of an unjust, unfair, or unpleasant situation. This meditation lets you shift your perspective so you experience more serenity—you may even change the dynamics of the relationship.

~~~~~

1 } Sit in a place where you feel comfortable and close your eyes. Take a deep breath and exhale. Do this two more times. Relax using whichever method you prefer.

2 } When you feel somewhat relaxed, mentally call to mind a situation about which you still harbor resentment, envy, anger, sadness, or other feelings that interfere with your peace of mind and contentment in a relationship with someone else. Mentally bring the situation into focus and allow yourself to really feel the unpleasant emotions associated with it.

3 } As you reexperience these emotions and the circumstances surrounding them, turn your head as far to the left as is comfortable for you. Let the remembered emotions reach a peak of clarity and intensity for you as you slowly inhale. Then, quickly turn your head to the right and exhale forcefully. "Blow away" the emotions connected with the situation along with your breath as you exhale.

4 } Feel the negative emotions and your attachment to the situation dispersing with your breath, as you send them far, far away from you. As you watch them disappear into the distance, you realize that they no longer have any meaning or power over you. You no longer need to cling to these memories from the past or give them space in your present-day life.

5 } Now, recall another situation that engenders resentment, envy, anger, or other feelings that interfere with your peace of mind. Allow yourself to really feel these unpleasant emotions as you turn your head to the left. When the remembered emotions reach a peak for you, inhale. Quickly turn your head to the right and exhale forcefully. "Blow away" the emotions connected with the situation along with your breath as you exhale.

(continued on page 156)

6 } Feel the negative emotions and your attachment to the situation dispersing as you send them far, far away from you. Continue in this manner for as long as you like, recalling situations that you associate with pain or unhappiness and releasing them with your breath.

7 } Feel the welcome release, peace, and contentment that come when you let go of these unpleasant emotions. Relax and enjoy this sense of serenity.

8 } When you feel you've done enough for one session, stop and open your eyes.

Ideally, you'll want to do this at the end of every day, releasing any and all unpleasant feelings and incidents that you've experienced during the day. It's also a good idea to gradually and systematically work back through your repertoire of old hurts, resentments, disappointments, and frustrations that involve other people, and to let them go by using this technique. Through letting go of old emotions, you allow forgiveness to heal old wounds and make room for new, positive experiences to take their place.

ACHIEVE WIN/WIN OUTCOMES

A "win/win" outcome is one in which both sides win. A compromise, requires both sides give up something. Obviously, a win/win outcome is preferable. Sometimes, however, ego issues, power struggles, or limited beliefs and vision can make it difficult for members of a partnership, team, committee, or group to create mutually beneficial results.

Even if none of us individually comprehends what is right for all concerned, our Higher Selves know. Your Higher Self, in partnership with everyone else's Higher Selves, can easily bring about success. The following meditation helps create win/win outcomes in your personal and professional relationships.

~~~~~~

1 } Sit or lie comfortably with your eyes closed. Take a deep breath and exhale. Do this two more times. Relax using whichever method you prefer. After you are relaxed, mentally count down from seven to one, relaxing more deeply with each count.

2 } On the count of one, find yourself in your Safe Place. Feel the beauty, love, blessed solitude, or enchantment of this place. Invite your Higher Self to join you. Sit together and talk of your desire to achieve a win/win outcome in a particular situation—a marriage, a business project, a team assignment, a legal proceeding, or something else.

3 } Now, invite into this Safe Place each individual involved in this particular situation, along with his/her Higher Self. You and your Higher Self and the other people and their Higher Selves form a circle. See or sense a beam of white light flowing from each Higher Self that con-verges in the center of the circle. At the point of convergence, a sphere of white light forms.

4 } You and the other members of the circle also send beams of white light to the center of the circle. Each beam adds to the central sphere of light. Sense the sphere becoming larger and larger until it is about 20 feet (6 m) in diameter. When it stops growing it begins to vibrate and radiate more light.

5 } Now everyone, Higher Selves included, enters into the sphere of light. Once inside, feel yourself being lifted higher and higher. Feel yourself expanding and transcending your physical self. Feel a loving connection with all the others in the group. This may be a powerful experience for you—let it happen.

6 } When you are ready, close your mental eyes and mentally count from one to five. On the count of five, open your physical eyes and return.

Do this meditation whenever you are involved in a negotiation, dispute, or other situation where a mutually beneficial resolution seems difficult.

According to Esther and Jerry Hicks' best-selling books about the Law of Attraction, your "point of attraction" is stronger when you're feeling good. The left frontal lobe of the brain tends to be more active in optimistic people. A University of Wisconsin study, reported in *WebMD Magazine* in 2009, showed increased electrical activity in the left frontal lobes of test subjects who underwent eight weeks of meditation training. These findings suggest that meditation can enhance your ability to attract the good things in life.

MEDITATIONS TO
ATTRACT WHAT YOU WANT IN LIFE

RECLAIM YOUR SELF-WORTH

Two studies in the *Journal of Experimental Social Psychology* in 2009 suggest that meditation can help people connect with and appreciate feelings of self-worth. The terms *self-esteem* and *self-worth* are often misunderstood. Self-esteem is an earned appreciation of yourself, a result of your actions and accomplishments. Self-worth is an ownership of your inherent value. It is your birthright. It is a constant. It can neither be added to nor taken away. You don't have to do anything to earn it. All you have to do is claim it. When you do, no dream, vision, or future will be beyond your grasp and no joy beyond your experience.

~~~~~

1 } Sit or lie comfortably, with your eyes closed. Take a deep breath and exhale. Do this two more times. Relax using whichever method you prefer. After you are somewhat relaxed, mentally count down from seven to one, relaxing more deeply with each count.

2 } On the count of one, find yourself in your Safe Place. Feel the beauty, love, blessed solitude, or enchantment of this place.

3 } Invite your Higher Self to join you. Sit together. Talk of your desire to reclaim your self-worth. When you are finished, invite your Inner Child (the one who hid his/her self-worth in order to protect it) to come and sit with you and your Higher Self.

4 } Hold your Inner Child. Love it. Ask your Inner Child to show you the secret place of your self-worth. Reassure your Inner Child that you will care for and cherish your self-worth and that s/he will be a part of you forever. When your Inner Child is reassured, s/he guides you and your Higher Self far beyond the Safe Place.

5 } In time, you arrive at an entrance, maybe in a wall, a hedge, or a grotto. On the other side of this entrance you come to a secret garden.

Enter the garden and explore. Feel the magic. Smell the fragrances. Hear the sounds. Marvel in the beauty, enchantment, blessed solitude, or love that permeates this place. Your Inner Child takes you to a secret hiding place within the garden. Maybe it is beneath a rock, or high in a tree. Maybe in an abandoned nest, or beneath the waters of a pool.

6 } Your Inner Child reaches into the hiding place and brings forth a dazzling, luminescent orb of white light. This is your self-worth, hidden and safe. Your Inner Child offers it to you. Take the shining orb and give it to your Higher Self. Your Higher Self takes from the orb another orb of luminescent white light and places it within your Inner Child's heart. Then your Higher Self places the first orb within your heart. Feel the light, the love, the joy flowing within and radiating about you.

7 } Lift your Inner Child and hold him/her in your arms. Your Higher Self will embrace you both in its arms. Let the magic happen. Now, close your mental eyes and mentally count from one to five. On the count of five, open your physical eyes and return, whole and valued.

ATTRACT OTHER PEOPLE INTO YOUR LIFE

This meditation opens opportunities for co-creating relationships that offer mutual success, happiness, growth, and learning. You can use it to attract a primary partner, clients, friends, a new baby, or even an animal companion.

Before beginning the meditation, decide only to bring into your life mutually beneficial relationships. Do not undertake this meditation to manipulate, dominate, or otherwise use others for one-sided gain or advantage. If you do so consciously or unconsciously, the meditation will not work. Your intention must always be to attract win-win relationships that provide maximum growth, healing, and well-being for all involved.

~~~~~~

1 } Sit or lie comfortably, with your eyes closed. Take a deep breath and exhale. Do this two more times. Relax using whichever method you prefer. After you are relaxed, mentally count down from seven to one, relaxing more deeply with each count.

2 } On the count of one, find yourself in your Safe Place. Take time to feel the beauty, love, blessed solitude, or enchantment of this place. Invite your Higher Self to join you. Sit together. Talk of your desire to attract someone into your life.

3 } When you have finished, your Higher Self draws into this place a mist or fog. It will become so thick you cannot see anything around you. Your Higher Self gently takes you by the hand and guides you through the mist/fog. When you reach the far side of the mist/fog, and it gradually drifts away, you find yourself standing with your Higher Self on a high, grassy mound at nighttime. Feel the silence, the beauty, the majesty of this place.

4 } Notice a tiny, luminescent sphere of light forming in your Higher Self's hand. It grows until it becomes a large orb of light. Imagine your desire as a sound, then blow it into the glowing orb. With your mind, lift the orb containing your desire higher and higher. Hear the sound resonating at a higher pitch as the orb rises into the night sky.

5 } Keep lifting the orb and the pitch higher and higher until they elevate beyond sight and hearing. When you are finished, thank your Higher Self.

6 } Close your mental eyes and mentally count from one to five.

7 } On the count of five, open your physical eyes and return.

Make ready for the arrival of the person you've attracted. Like a radio tuned to a certain station, that person will pick up the sound you released into the airwaves and follow it to you. You only need to do this meditation once—after you send out the call, be patient.

DEVELOP AN ATTITUDE OF GRATITUDE

People with positive attitudes are healthier and live longer than pessimists, according to a study presented at the American Psychosomatic Society's annual meeting in 2009. The Women's Health Initiative conducted a clinical trial of 97,000 women, age fifty to seventy-four, and after eight years found the risk of death from any cause was 14 percent lower for the women with positive attitudes.

The old adage of counting your blessings and trying to see the glass as half-full rather than half-empty really can boost optimism. The following practice helps you develop an attitude of gratitude, so you can attract greater health, happiness, and other blessings in life.

1 } Purchase or make a journal. If you like, decorate it with positive images.

2 } Each morning, spend several minutes thinking about something in your life for which you feel grateful—friends, family, health, a job you like, your pet, and so on.

3 } Spend a few minutes writing in your journal about one or more of these things. Keep your thoughts focused on what you're writing— don't let your mind drift to other thoughts, especially worries or negative ideas.

4 } As you write, allow yourself to feel thankful and glad that these things are in your life. Focus on the pleasant feelings that arise as you count your blessings. If you wish, write or say "thank you."

5 } Before going to bed at night, write in your journal at least one good thing that happened to you during the day. It could be something as simple as seeing a flower blooming or receiving a smile from a stranger in the supermarket.

6 } Notice how your emotions start to lift as you shift your thoughts into positive mode. Thoughts trigger emotions, not the other way around.

7 } Whenever you start to feel discouraged or cynical, open your journal and read a few of the positive experiences you've recorded there.

Do this daily. By training your mind to focus on the good around you, rather than the bad, you shift your awareness and invite more positive things to come your way.

CHANGE YOUR PERCEPTIONS TO CHANGE YOUR REALITY

Quantum physics shows us that when we focus our attention on something, we actually influence the movement of the molecules that comprise it. As the Heisenberg Uncertainty Principle revealed, the observer affects what's being observed. Therefore, it stands to reason that if you continue to see things in a particular way, you hold them in place and prevent change.

This meditation lets you shift your perspective so you no longer feel attached to an idea, emotion, or outcome. You will become an objective witness to your thoughts and feelings, rather than identifying with them. In so doing, you release "stuck" energy and allow it to move freely, opening the way for new possibilities to enter your life.

~~~~~~

1} Sit comfortably in a quiet place where you feel safe. Close your eyes, and begin breathing slowly and deeply. Become aware of how you are sitting. Notice any parts of your body that feel tense, such as your lower back or shoulders.

2} Bring your attention to those parts of your body, one at a time, and gradually allow them to soften. Continue breathing slowly and deeply as you feel your body relax. When you are ready, bring to mind an idea or emotion to which you feel attached. It may be one you've held onto for a very long time. Your attachment to this idea or emotion is keeping you stuck in a particular pattern. It blocks you from experiencing peace and contentment, and prevents you from attracting the blessings you seek.

3} Instead of analyzing, judging, defending, or intellectualizing about this idea or emotion, imagine you are watching it on a TV screen. See or sense yourself sitting in a chair across the room, simply observing what's happening on the TV. The scenario you see on the TV depicts a particular idea or emotion you have held on to up until now.

4} Although this scenario is what's playing on this channel, you have hundreds of channels you can watch, and something different is playing on each of them. If you choose, you can take control of the TV and change what you see.

5} Imagine picking up the remote control and changing the channel. What you see now depicts another scenario. It represents another way of experiencing things, one that's different from your old idea or emotion.

(continued on page 166)

6 } Change channels again. And again. Observe how many different possibilities exist. You realize you are not limited to only one "reality" just as you are not limited to watching only one program. Play around with the possibilities. Channel surf, allowing yourself to observe and explore many different options. You can even turn the TV off if you choose.

7 } Continue in this manner for as long as you like. When you feel ready, slowly open your eyes.

Do this meditation often for at least ten minutes at a time to help you detach from troubling thoughts, emotions, situations, or people. Deal with one issue at a time and practice separating yourself from it, before attempting to address another issue. By releasing your attachments, you reduce the suffering that comes from striving to control people and situations that are really out of your control. Letting go of fixed ideas and attitudes also helps pave the way for new opportunities to come into your life.

SHIFT YOUR PERSPECTIVE TO SEE NEW OPPORTUNITIES

Best-selling author Dr. Wayne Dyer is fond of saying, "When you change the way you look at things, the things you look at change." It's easy to get stuck in old patterns of thinking that limit your ability to see new possibilities. Meditation calms the mind and expands your awareness, enabling you to envision a broader range of options. It also lets you delve into your subconscious to gain insight into problems and get answers your analytic, rational brain might have missed.

The following meditation expands your ordinary perspective. It allows you to experiment with seeing life from different vantage points and alerts you to possibilities you may not have realized before.

~~~~~~

1 } Sit comfortably in a quiet place where you feel safe. Close your eyes, and begin breathing slowly and deeply. Relax using whichever method you prefer. When you feel ready, turn your attention to the outer surface of your physical body. With your mind's eye, trace the outline of your physical body. Slide your gaze along your arms, legs, torso, and head. Notice where your body stops and your clothing begins. If you are seated in a chair, become aware of where your body contacts the material of the chair, where your feet touch the floor. Observe where the skin of your face, your hair, and your hands meet the air.

2 } Now, imagine your life energy as an opalescent, milky-white light glowing within you. Allow the light to expand gently through the top of your head. You are not constrained within the boundaries of your physical body. Sense this energy pushing upward and outward, until it extends about 6 inches (15 cm) beyond and around your head, like a halo. Now, shift your attention to your feet. Feel your light-energy expanding through the soles of your feet, until it extends about 6 inches (15 cm) beyond your physical feet. Imagine your whole body gradually swelling like a balloon.

3 } Sense your light-energy expanding about 6 inches (15 cm) beyond the ordinary boundaries of your skin. You may notice a slight tingling sensation on the surface of your body or around it as you stretch beyond the body's ordinary limitations. Sense a bubble of glowing white light-energy—your energy—completely surrounding your physical body. Let your mind perceive this for a few moments, until it feels comfortable for you. Now, shift your attention to a spot between your shoulder blades and about 6 inches (15 cm) out from the center of your back. This is what's sometimes called the "assemblage point." Your view of the world is centered in this place, not your eyes. From here, you see things straight ahead, in a somewhat "blinkered" manner.

(continued on page 168)

4 } Mentally slide the assemblage point about 2 feet (61 cm) up and to the right. Notice that now you perceive the world from a slightly different angle, from above your right shoulder instead of straight on. How do things look from here? Next, mentally move your assemblage point to the left, until you are about 2 feet (61 cm) above and to the left of your starting point. Notice how the world appears from this vantage point above your left shoulder. Do you see things you've missed before? Can you see a new possibility or a different route you could take from here?

5 } Practice shifting your assemblage point. Experiment with observing things from various angles. As you shift your assemblage point, notice how your perceptions of the world around you change. By now, you realize that nothing is fixed. The situations you experience are not objective. In a sense, what you see is what you get. By changing your view of a situation or experience, you can change it to attract whatever you'd like to instead.

6 } You can shift your assemblage point any time you wish, in order to get a different perspective. You can change your experience of your life at will. Shifting your assemblage point lets you see new possibilities and opportunities. You realize you are trapped only by your perceptions, not by circumstances outside you. Experiment with shifting your assemblage point and receiving information for as long as you like.

7 } When you feel ready, slowly open your eyes and return.

Practice this meditation whenever you wish to move beyond self-imposed restrictions and see things from a different perspective. By expanding your vision, you become receptive to new ideas, people, and opportunities.

USE A CRYSTAL TO ATTRACT PROSPERITY

One of our great advances in the twentieth century was learning to harness the incredible power of quartz crystals. From applications such as crystal radios to high-powered computer technology, this knowledge has propelled us into an unlimited future. Quartz possesses unique abilities: it can gather, store, and release energy; it can amplify and direct that energy; with laserlike precision it can send information anywhere. It can also attract whatever you program into it, and like a honing beam draw it to you. You can use the meditation below to attract prosperity—or anything else you desire.

~~~~~~

BEFORE YOU BEGIN

1 } First, find a crystal with which to work. We recommend choosing a quartz crystal that contains chlorite inclusions, sometimes called an "abundance crystal." The tiny mineral particles within the crystal give it a greenish color. If you cannot find an abundance crystal, any quartz crystal will do. We suggest using a crystal no smaller than 2 inches (5 cm) in diameter or no less than 2 inches (5 cm) in length.

2 } After you've acquired your crystal, hold it under running, tepid water to clean it. Then rub your thumb sharply across each side, blowing sharply over the crystal as you rub it. The rubbing and blowing must be simultaneous. This "releases" any programs that the crystal's previous keepers may have put there, as well as any "gunk" that may have collected within it.

3 } Now, mentally instruct the crystal that your intention is to draw prosperity to you. Hold this intention in your mind and blow it into the crystal with a quick, short breath. The crystal is now ready to do its work, and you are ready to meditate.

THE MEDITATION

1 } Hold the crystal in one or both hands. Take a deep breath and exhale. Do this two more times. Sit or lie comfortably, with your eyes closed. Relax using whichever method you prefer. After you are relaxed, mentally count down from seven to one, relaxing more deeply with each count.

2 } On the count of one, find yourself in your Safe Place. See or sense yourself sitting in your Safe Place, holding the crystal. Gaze into the crystal. Marvel at its beauty, its majesty. Notice its inner world of color and light. Marvel at the amazing wisps, clouds, colors, or sparkling inclusions it may possess.

3 } Now, take a deep breath. As you exhale, imagine yourself inside the crystal. Explore its inner world. Marvel at the beauty and majesty there. While sitting inside the crystal, imagine having (not getting) the prosperity you desire. Picture it as a single moment, not as a series of events.

(continued on page 170)

4 } Feel what it would be like having this prosperity. Feel the joy, the satisfaction, the exhilaration of having received it. The more you charge the crystal with your feelings, the greater your ability to attract what you desire through it. Amplify your feelings—really let yourself go.

5 } Now, use your imagination to place this mental "picture" within the heart of the crystal. When you have done this, take a deep breath.

6 } As you exhale, see or sense yourself outside the crystal again. Thank the crystal for working with you to accomplish your goals.

7 } Close your mental eyes and mentally count from one to five. On the count of five, open your physical eyes and return.

The crystal will do the work you've programmed it to do. But, every now and then, sit and hold the crystal for a while. "Charge" it with your feelings and your intention. Let the magic happen.

CLARIFY YOUR OBJECTIVES TO ATTRACT WHAT YOU DESIRE

When you order something from a catalog or online, you must clearly stipulate what you want—item number, size, color, quantity, and so on. The same holds true when you "order" something from the universe. If you aren't clear about what you intend to attract, you may end up with something you didn't expect or want.

Meditation enables you to eliminate confusion, focus your mind, and clarify your intentions. In a 2006 *Time* magazine article, Wall Street whiz Walter Zimmermann said that meditation helps him "maintain the clarity he needs for quick, insightful analysis." Use the following practice to clarify your objectives and attract what you truly desire.

1 } Contemplate what you wish to attract into your life: money, good health, a loving relationship, career success, a beautiful home, or something else. Consider all the details involved in your goal. For instance, if your objective is to find the ideal job, think about the specific factors you desire: salary, responsibilities, location, schedule, work environment, and so on.

2 } Write your objective on a piece of paper, using clear, simple, unambiguous language. In your description, include everything you desire—be specific. State your intentions in a positive manner and in the present tense, as if you already have what you desire.

3 } When you've finished, sit quietly in a place where you feel safe and comfortable, and close your eyes. Breathe slowly and deeply, as you allow your mind and body to relax. Form an image in your mind of what it is you seek—a home, job, car, relationship, or other object or situation. Make your vision as clear and vivid as possible. See and/or sense it as best you can. Include all the details you noted in your written description.

4 } Imagine yourself enjoying the object of your desire. Envision yourself driving the car, living in the house, or performing the job you seek. Enrich your vision with details and emotion. Allow yourself to imagine at length how you'll feel having reaped the benefits of your desire.

5 } If other thoughts intrude, gently ease them aside. If your mind starts to wander, bring it back to your intention. Don't let doubt or fear diminish your enthusiasm. Be confident that what you see in your mind's eye will appear in the physical world, at the right time. Spend as much time as you like imagining the object or situation you wish to attract.

6 } When you feel ready, open your eyes and return. In a safe place, burn the paper on which you wrote your objective.

7 } As the paper disintegrates, imagine your wishes are being released into the universe. Your request will now attract whatever it is you desire. Express gratitude, as if you already have what you desire.

ATTRACT WHATEVER YOU DESIRE—WHILE YOU SLEEP

A study conducted in connection with the University of Calgary in Alberta, Canada, and published in *Psychosomatic Medicine* in 2003, examined 101 men and women to see how meditation affected their quality of life. At the end of the eight-week study, significant improvements were observed in many areas, including the participants' sleep quality.

Your mind never sleeps. Even during deep sleep, when the brain is in the delta state, it is actively healing you and integrating experiences more effectively than is possible when you are awake. Although you're not aware of what's actually taking place, you can choose what you want your unconscious to work on while you sleep. You can program your mind to attract health, prosperity, a relationship—whatever you desire.

1 } Just before falling asleep, decide what you want to work on while you sleep. Do you seek healing? Is there something you want to learn more about or an issue you wish to resolve? Would you like to manifest something in your life? Be specific.

2 } Hold the desire in your mind as you drift off to sleep. Visualize the desire. Feel it.

3 } When you wake in the morning, immediately write down what you remember of any dreams you may have had. If you like, draw pictures of what you can recall.

Do this every night before falling asleep. You may not remember your dreams at first—it takes a little practice. Writing down what you recall of your dreams first thing each morning trains your mind to get into the habit of remembering. Whether or not you remember a dream, the programming will have an effect. In time, you'll become aware of it and see results.

TAP THE ATTRACTING POWER OF SEX

According to Tantric Yoga, a spiritual practice used in the East for 6,000 years, sexual orgasm is one of the most powerful forces we can experience. It is considered to be very close to the frequency of divine bliss. Holding an intention in your mind during this moment of peak experience "fuels" your intention and increases your ability to attract whatever you want in life. This waking meditation will be far more effective if you practice it with someone you love.

In their book *The 7 Secrets of Synchronicity*, Trish and Rob MacGregor explain it this way: "When we are focused, passionate, pushing our limits, our brains release endorphins. Research indicates this happens during sex, childbirth, strenuous exercise, meditation, and intense creative work. If you visualize what you want when endorphins are rushing through you, desires manifest more quickly. It's as if the endorphins somehow help connect you to the powerful source of who you really are, and the potential of who you can become."

~~~~~~~

1 } Before undertaking this meditation, discuss with your partner what one, or both, of you wish to attract—a new job, a home, good health, whatever you desire. Choose only one thing at a time. It's important that you are very clear about your objective and in agreement.

2 } Engage in sex. Take your time and make the act an expression of your mutual love. Feel love's tenderness, the divine dance of ebb and flow, the blending of two energy forces becoming one.

3 } As you approach climax, hold in your minds a mental image of what you intend to attract.

4 } As you reach orgasm, feel the joy of having received your wish, and then release it. The force of your physical release propels your intention out into the universe like a rocket.

5 } Let the image totally go. Do not think about or discuss your intention. Relax; enjoy each other and the blissful state of calm that follows.

Perform this practice as often as you like. The more time you invest in raising your level of excitement and pleasure, the better. You may choose the same intention each time, or something different. Don't doubt or worry about whether your wish will materialize—just enjoy yourselves. (For more information, see Skye's forthcoming book, *Easy Sex Magic*.)

DAYDREAM YOUR WAY TO FULFILLMENT

In their best-selling books about the Law of Attraction, Esther and Jerry Hicks emphasize the importance of daydreaming on a daily basis in order to attract whatever you want in life. When you daydream, your brain waves shift into the alpha state—the same level of consciousness you tap when you meditate. The key is to daydream with intention, not to let your mind drift about randomly.

~~~~~

1 } Sit or lie comfortably, with your eyes closed. Take a deep breath and exhale. Do this two more times. Relax using whichever method you prefer.

2 } Bring to mind something you wish to attract into your life—a beautiful home, good health, a relationship, a new car, whatever you desire.

3 } Think about the various aspects of what you desire. If you're seeking a home of your own, for example, imagine the things you'd like to have in that home: a fireplace, a gourmet kitchen, gleaming wooden floors, lavishly appointed bathrooms, a spacious deck, a big garage with a workshop—anything you want. Dream big.

4 } Include as much detail and richness as you can. Give your imagination free rein.

5 } Get your emotions involved in your daydream. Feel the thrill of driving up to your new home the first time. Enjoy cooking in your gourmet kitchen and serving meals to friends and family members. Experience the comfort of sitting in front of your fireplace on a cool evening. See yourself sitting on your patio or working in your garden.

6 } Have fun. The more joy you bring into the experience, the faster you'll achieve the outcome you desire—and the more positive that outcome will be.

7 } When you're ready, open your eyes.

Daydream in this manner for at least ten minutes a day, until you receive the outcome you desire. Then, work on fulfilling another wish.

WRITE YOUR WAY TO SUCCESS

Years ago, Skye did a series of talks with other writers about a phenomenon they considered (at the time) to be a bit odd. It seemed that frequently when they wrote about something in one of their books, it later happened in their real lives. At the time, none of the writers realized that he or she was actively engaging the creative process to attract situations. In fact, writing is a very effective way to focus your imagination to produce results. Try it and see.

~~~~~~

1 } Acquire a notebook or journal that you'll use for this purpose only. Use a pen and paper—don't keyboard at your computer. Holding the pen activates acupressure points in your fingertips that send signals to your brain.

2 } Bring to mind something you wish to attract into your life—a new job, a relationship, a home, whatever you desire.

3 } Write down everything you can think of related to your desire. Bring in as much detail as possible. If you're seeking a new job, for example, describe the tasks you'd perform at that job. Discuss the exciting challenges you'd face and the things you'd learn at your job. Write about the environment where you'd work and what you'd wear. What products or services would you offer? What tools or equipment would you use? Who are your coworkers and/or customers? Will you travel to places in connection with your employment? What hours will you keep?

4 } Stay focused on your writing. The physical act of writing helps prevent your mind from wandering. It also invites your subconscious to present all sorts of information that can be useful in fine-tuning your desires.

5 } Now, write about your successes and accomplishments in your job. Describe the recognition and respect you get from coworkers, colleagues, bosses, and clients. Jot down your sense of satisfaction at being good at what you do. Write about winning awards and honors. Discuss receiving a big paycheck, bonuses, commissions, and other forms of compensation.

6 } Be sure to write in the first person and in the present tense, as if you already have the job you seek and are already doing it successfully.

7 } As you write, feel the enjoyment of performing the job you desire. Experience the satisfaction of success.

Do this waking meditation every day. Fill at least one complete page per sitting, more if you like, until you've received what you set out to attract. When you've attracted one thing on your list of wishes, start writing about another, using the same technique.

THE MOST POWERFUL MEDITATION EVER (AND THE MOST DIFFICULT)

The following meditation is the most powerful meditation, or technique, you will ever perform. When done from a place of integrity (meaning being the adult you are, not the child or adolescent you may sometimes play), this meditation can attract anything you desire into your life or release anything from it that you don't want. How does the meditation work? It employs a fundamental secret of life: Whatever it is you ask for, the answer is always "yes." The key is knowing what you are really *asking for*. Sometimes, what you consciously seek conflicts with what you unconsciously desire. (We discussed this more fully in part 1.) In such instances, your unconscious will win out.

~~~~~~~

1 } Instead of viewing success as a reward or failure as punishment, this meditation asks you to see life as a gift. The only requirement is that you allow yourself to receive the gift and let it unfold.

2 } Sit or lie comfortably, with your eyes closed. Take a deep breath and exhale. Do this two more times. Relax using whichever method you prefer. After you are relaxed, mentally count down from seven to one, relaxing more deeply with each count.

3 } On the count of one, find yourself in your Safe Place. Feel the beauty, love, blessed solitude, or enchantment of this place. Invite your Higher Self to join you.

4 } With integrity and sincerity—and without desperation, self-pity, or doubt—ask your Higher Self for help.

5 } Be willing to receive the help you've requested. Don't try to direct, judge, or predict how the help will come or how your request will materialize. Just allow it to do so.

6 } When you feel ready, close your mental eyes and mentally count from one to five.

7 } On the count of five, open your physical eyes and return.

Some people find this meditation so effective and powerful it frightens them, and they stop doing it. You may wish to start small—ask for something to which you don't have a strong emotional attachment. As you grow more comfortable with attracting what you request, you can ask for things that are more important to you.

When you meditate, you access the right hemisphere of the brain—the part that governs imagination, intuition, and creativity. Meditation also quiets your "inner judge"—the voice of discouragement that can block creative attempts. Therefore, it's not surprising that three studies of more than three hundred students, published in the journal *Intelligence*, found meditation increased their creativity.

MEDITATIONS TO
AID CREATIVITY, INTELLIGENCE, AND PROBLEM SOLVING

NIGHT WHISPERS: GAIN CREATIVE INSPIRATION AT NIGHT

Nighttime has long been associated with intuition, imagination, mystery, and the unconscious realm. In many spiritual traditions, the moon represents the feminine deity and her creative power. A study done at Catholic University of the Sacred Heart's Department of Psychology in Milan, Italy, and presented in a Discovery Channel TV program in 2006, found that "night owls" tend to be creative thinkers.

Sitting outside under the canopy of a night sky can certainly get the creative juices flowing. The stillness and solitude are perfect for awakening creativity and inspiration. The magic in the night air seems to bathe away any blocks and resistances you may be experiencing, and the stars and moon serve as steady allies in this waking meditation. Devote a few evenings, weather allowing, to sitting outside in silence without distractions.

~~~~~

1 } Sit quietly. Close your eyes for a little while and allow the stillness to quiet your mental noise. Feel your heartbeat settling into a calm, easy pace. Your breathing becomes slower, deeper, more refined.

2 } You may feel some restlessness temporarily. That's okay. If you're not used to being alone outside at night the experience may seem strange or even a little scary at first. Also, this experience challenges the blockages that are interfering with your creativity and inspiration. Give it time; the uneasiness will pass.

3 } Open your eyes when you feel ready. Just sit, quietly. Feel the peace, the softness, the grandeur that is Night. Gaze at the moon and stars.

Let them speak to you. Feel a connection with the universe and everything in it. In time, when the mental noise is quieted, the Night will work its magic. Ideas, inspirations, resolutions, and insights will start flowing. Flow with them.

4 } Don't try to control what presents itself to you; just let whatever comes, come. On your notepad, jot down what comes to you, so you won't forget later. Don't censor what presents itself to you; just note it and keep your mind open.

5 } Spend as long as you like experiencing the magical, mystical energy of the Night and your own awakening inspiration. When you're ready to "call it an evening," thank the Night, and go indoors.

Most likely, you'll experience some resistance at first. This is normal—don't fight it. It may take a night or two, but eventually the resistance will end. Do this waking meditation for at least an hour each night in order to free your imagination and dissolve creative blocks.

LET NATURE INSPIRE CREATIVITY AND ANSWERS

Modern Westerners have lost an ability our ancestors long ago possessed: the ability to "read" everyday things around us and to glean answers from them. Our ancestors knew that nature provided not only for our basic needs but also the answers to life's mysteries and our mundane questions as well. Animal behavior, weather patterns, and other symbols in nature offered insights and inspiration.

Although this ability to read nature has atrophied in most people, you can once again strengthen your receptivity and awareness of the world around you and learn to see nature as a most amazing oracle. The following meditation, which derives from an ancient Scottish tradition, will help you reawaken this lost ability. (See Skye's *The Everything Spells & Charms Book* and Ted Andrews's *Animal-Speak* for more information about developing this nature-based oracle and your own intuition.)

1} In the morning as soon as you wake up, bring to mind a question, problem, or situation about which you'd like more insight or information. Take a few deep breaths to calm and center yourself, as you move from a sleeping state to waking consciousness. Keep your mind relaxed and open—don't start thinking about what you have to do today.

2} While holding your question or concern in your mind, step outside. The first thing that captures your attention offers an answer or guidance. It may be a bird, a flower, a cloud, or something else. Whatever it is, observe it as objectively as possible. What do you notice about it? What is it doing? How do you feel about it or its behavior?

3} Notice any emotions, sensations, or impressions that arise within you in connection with what you see. When you feel ready, go back inside.

4} Spend a few minutes thinking about what this sighting means to you. Do you have any personal connections to what you've seen? Did you feel happy, sad, or anxious?

5} Consider the symbolism associated with whatever you've observed. If you spotted an animal or a bird, think about its characteristics, behavior, habitat, and so on—how do they relate to your question or concern? If you noticed a tree or plant, what was its stage of development? Was it budding, in full bloom, dropping its leaves as winter approaches, or barren? Colors, numbers, and other symbols may also be significant.

6 } Respect your intuition and any feelings you have regarding what you've seen. Remember, this is a highly personal experience, and although other sources may provide interpretations or suggestions, your own impressions are what matter most.

7 } If you feel your sighting has provided insight into your question or concern, that's great. If not, write down what you saw and allow the experience to gestate. In time, you'll receive the answer or information you seek.

Do this meditation whenever you seek an answer or insight into an issue. You may also use this meditation to gain inspiration, direction, or ideas for a creative undertaking—let what you observe serve as a starting point for an endeavor.

INCREASE INSPIRATION AND INGENUITY

Edgar Cayce, known as the "Sleeping Prophet," had only an eighth-grade education and no medical training, yet he discovered cures for thousands of ailing people. He accomplished this by going into a trancelike state and connecting with the wisdom of physicians, scientists, and others who were no longer living on Earth (for more information, see www.edgarcayce.org).

What if you could consult with the Masters—living or dead—who most inspire you? What if their mastery could influence you? You probably won't be able to "download" information as Cayce did, but you can gain insights and strengthen your own abilities. Consider taking a walk with Thoreau, Emerson, or Shakespeare, or having lunch with Picasso, Rembrandt, or Monet. What if Dylan Thomas, Emily Dickinson, or Robert Frost whispered in your ear while you worked on your next poem? How about solving problems with Einstein, Galileo, or Kepler? This meditation lets you explore those possibilities and more. What might the great Masters tell you? What would you ask them? How would your work change? How would you change? Why not find out?

~~~~~~

1 } Make a list of up to ten people, living or dead, with whom you would like to consult. Choose men and women whose work you most admire, who most inspire you. Now go into meditation.

2 } Sit or lie comfortably, with your eyes closed. Take a deep breath and exhale. Do this two more times. Relax using whichever method you prefer. After you are relaxed, mentally count down from seven to one, relaxing more deeply with each count.

3 } On the count of one, find yourself in your Safe Place. Feel the beauty, love, blessed solitude, or enchantment of this place.

4 } When you feel ready, invite one or more of these Masters to join you. When they arrive, sit together and talk. Speak to them of your work, your dreams, your passions. Ask them for their counsel. They will all agree to assist you. Some of the Masters you've selected might have had attitudes, habits, or other qualities while in human form that you don't particularly like. However, you are sitting with their Truer Selves now, not with the human beings they were in their physical lives on Earth.

5 } Listen as they offer their input. You may experience this as words, feelings, ideas, or mental pictures. Receive their counsel in whatever way it comes. When they've finished sharing their insights with you, thank them and ask for their continued counsel. They will agree.

6 } The Masters now return to where they came from before joining you. You can meet with them again whenever you choose.

7 } Now, close your mental eyes and mentally count from one to five.

8 } On the count of five, open your physical eyes and return.

Commit to meeting with the Masters on a regular basis, perhaps once per week, once every two weeks, once a month—whatever is comfortable for you. Work with these Masters meditatively and non-meditatively. When you are writing, painting, composing, or conducting business, invite them to join you. Remain open to their counsel. Receive their input and inspiration. Communing with the Masters will become easier over time—and as you learn from them, your creativity and ingenuity will become more brilliant.

UNBLOCK YOUR CREATIVITY

In her groundbreaking book, *The Artist's Way*, author Julia Cameron introduces an exercise she calls "Morning Pages." This highly effective procedure opens vast reservoirs of creativity and self-understanding. It also provides opportunities for healing emotional wounds that can block your creativity or interfere with other parts of your life. Through a simple process of spontaneous writing, you may discover deep-seated beliefs and self-limiting perceptions long hidden from your awareness—and, if you choose, eliminate them.

Martin incorporates this exercise into many of his counseling sessions and finds it stimulates significant changes in his clients' emotional, physical, and mental well-being. The process enables you to integrate all aspects of yourself, so you become more creative, self-aware, and fulfilled.

1 } Set aside time each day to do the exercise. It's ideal to do this first thing in the morning, but if that's not possible, do it when you can. It's important, however, that you do it daily.

2 } Using a pen and notebook, write three full pages about whatever comes to mind.

3 } This is *not* journaling or diary writing—just let your thoughts flow freely. Don't concern yourself with spelling or grammar. Write whatever pops into your mind, even if it's not coherent or logical.

4 } Don't type/keyboard or dictate your thoughts into a tape recorder. The physical act of writing is necessary to the process because the movement of your hand and the pressure of the pen/pencil on your fingertips trigger certain key brain responses.

5 } This whole process may seem difficult at first. You might find yourself sitting and staring at the paper for several minutes. You may even experience frustration initially. That's okay, but don't give up. After a while, thoughts will come and the words will start to flow.

6 } If negative feelings or thoughts come up, which can happen in the beginning, don't push them back down—allow yourself to feel them and express them. Whatever comes up, don't censor it; write it out. These feelings may be connected to your creative blocks. In time, your emotions will become lighter.

7 } You'll notice that what is expressed in the writing addresses you personally. It may seem as if a part of yourself is speaking to you about you. These are the beliefs you hold about yourself. Once you acknowledge these beliefs, you can change them if you choose.

Do this practice every day. Julia Cameron recommends committing to this activity for a minimum of three months. Spend as long it takes. Write no less and no more than three pages per day. Let no one else read what you have written—not your spouse, your best friend, or even your therapist. By keeping what you write completely private, you feel free to express whatever you need to express without fear of censorship or judgment.

THE ANSWER BOX:
RESOLVE PROBLEMS, GET ANSWERS

Daily meditation, as Sara Lazar, PhD, and fellow researchers at Massachusetts General Hospital discovered in 2005, actually thickens the parts of the brain's cerebral cortex that are responsible for decision making. In addition, meditation taps the creative, intuitive right hemisphere of the brain, enabling you to gain insight in a way left-brain rational thinking can't.

Sometimes answers elude us when we struggle to solve our problems using a head-on approach. If you feel stumped, a more relaxed method may produce the results you seek. That's what happens when you "sleep on it"—your dreams often provide answers your conscious mind missed. This meditation draws on the rituals of ancient peoples—including the Egyptians, Maya, Chinese, and Tibetans—who buried boxes filled with prayers and other requests in the earth in order to gain answers and assistance.

~~~~~~

1 } Find an old, antique-looking box with a lid. Use this box only for the purposes described in this meditation. Consider it your "Answer Box."

2 } On a piece of paper write a question, a problem, or an issue for which you'd like an answer or guidance. Fold the paper and place it in your Answer Box.

3 } Now, prepare to go into meditation. Sit or lie comfortably, with your eyes closed. Take a deep breath and exhale. Do this two more times. Relax using whichever method you prefer.

4 } When you feel relaxed, mentally count down from seven to one, relaxing more deeply with each count. On the count of one, find yourself in a beautiful garden. Trees and flowers of all kinds delight your senses. Perhaps you see a stream or fountain. You may notice birds, butterflies, or animals here as well. Let this be a place of enchantment for you. In your hands you hold a box. This box contains the piece of paper on which you've written your question, problem, or request. Gaze about the garden until you spot a place where you can bury the box. With your hands, start digging a hole in the earth.

5 } Place the box carefully in the ground, and then cover it with dirt. By burying the box, you are allowing your concern to gestate—like a seed planted in the soil—until it's ready to burst forth in blossom at a later date.

6 } When you've finished, close your mental eyes and sit quietly. Then, mentally count from one to five. On the count of five, open your physical eyes and return.

7 } Take the box with your written request in it and secret it someplace in your home—a closet, the basement or attic, or another place where it will be hidden from view.

Your answer or guidance will come either while you are in meditation or shortly thereafter. The first thing that comes to you, after you come out of meditation or finish storing the box safely, may lead to the answer you seek. If you turn on the radio or TV, for instance, the first thing you hear could answer your question. If you look at a newspaper or open a book, the first thing you read will offer guidance. If an answer does not come immediately, it soon will, often within one to three days. Look for it. Pay attention. Be open. When you receive the answer, take the paper out of the Answer Box and burn it.

WATCH CLOUDS TO EXPAND CREATIVITY AND IMAGINATION

When you were a child, you probably watched clouds drifting by and imagined them changing into myriad shapes. This enjoyable meditative practice is more than a youthful amusement, however—it can actually expand your creative ability. That's because meditation slows brain wave function, while letting you temporarily sidestep ordinary analytic thinking, so you can tap into the intuitive, creative part of your brain. A study of 362 Taiwanese students, published in the journal *Intelligence* in 2001, found that meditation improved their creativity and perceptual functions. Do the following meditation to help you think outside the box and arrive at creative solutions to problems.

1 } Lie on your back outdoors, in a place where you feel comfortable.

2 } Relax and empty your mind of thoughts as you gaze up at the sky. Choose a cloud and observe it calmly. Do you perceive images or shapes in it? Does it look like an animal, a car, a tree, or something else?

3 } As the cloud drifts across the sky, watch it slowly change shape. What does it remind you of now?

4 } Keep observing the cloud as it shifts its shape again and again. Give your imagination free rein.

5 } Choose another cloud and watch it transform itself into various images. What do they look like to you?

6 } If other thoughts arise into your awareness, simply let them go and focus your attention again on the clouds.

7 } Continue doing this for as long as you like.

Spend at least ten minutes watching clouds to relax your mind and allow your imagination to flow freely.

EXPAND YOUR LEARNING CAPACITY

A two-year study, published in the journal *Personality and Individual Differences* in 1991, examined one hundred university students to see if meditation could influence their learning ability and IQ scores. Researchers found that students who meditated twice daily performed better than non-meditators on standardized intelligence tests. A more recent study of fifty college students, reported in the *International Journal of Psychophysiology* in 2009, confirmed earlier findings. After only ten weeks, students who meditated scored significantly higher on the Brain Integration Scale (see page 118 for more information on this scale).

The following meditation helps expand your learning capacity by removing distractions and inconsequential material that clutter your brain.

~~~~~~

1 } Sit in a quiet place where you feel comfortable. Close your eyes, and begin breathing slowly and deeply.

2 } For a few moments, notice the numerous thoughts that flit through your mind. Simply observe them, without responding to them or giving them your attention.

3 } Now, imagine these thoughts as tiny bits of litter, dust, or dirt spilled on the floor all around you. See or sense yourself picking up a vacuum cleaner and turning it on.

4 } Begin vacuuming up all the litter/dirt from the floor. As the vacuum cleaner sucks up the litter/dirt, sense all the clutter and miscella- neous random and inconsequential thoughts being gently removed from your mind.

5 } Feel your mind growing calmer as all the distractions are cleared away. Enjoy the sense of clarity and spaciousness that results. As thoughts arise into your awareness, simply vacuum them up. Continue vacuuming until all the litter, dust, or dirt has been removed.

6 } As the clutter disappears from your mind, you find you have more room to accommodate new, useful knowledge and information. Your mind is relaxed, receptive, and open.

7 } When you feel ready, open your eyes.

Do this meditation for at least five minutes periodically during the day to clear away unwanted thoughts. You can also do this as a waking meditation. Whenever you vacuum your home, imagine you are removing mental clutter along with the physical dust and dirt. Keep your attention focused on your chore, instead of letting your mind wander.

STEP OUTSIDE YOUR SELF-IMPOSED LIMITS

Pierre Teilhard de Chardin, French anthropologist, priest, philosopher, and mystic, wrote, "Our duty, as men and women, is to proceed as if limits to our ability did not exist. We are collaborators in creation." Many of us limit ourselves unnecessarily. Often the beliefs and behaviors we think protect us actually imprison us. This meditation helps you step outside your self-imposed limits and discover new possibilities for yourself.

1 } Stand in a comfortable position, with your arms at your sides and your feet about shoulder-width apart. Close your eyes. If necessary, hold on to something to maintain your balance. Take a deep breath and exhale. Do this two more times.

2 } Imagine a circular wall surrounding you, at least a foot (30 cm) taller than you are, so you can't see over it. See or sense yourself standing in the center of the circle. The circle is so small that if you stretch out your arms in any direction you can touch the wall. Your vision and movement are limited to the space inside the circle.

3 } Take a few moments to experience the constriction and confinement of being within this enclosed space. Feel how cramped and limited your existence is within this tight circle. Now, try to imagine what might lie outside this circle. Allow your curiosity to rise.

4 } Reach out and touch the wall. Notice that it really isn't very substantial. Realize, too, that you are the one who erected this wall and you can choose to go beyond it. When you're ready, point your index finger at the wall.

5 } With your finger, imagine cutting a doorway in the wall large enough for you to walk through. See or sense yourself pushing the door open. Take a step forward and walk through the door, out into the big, bright world beyond. Feel the freedom, excitement, and joy of being outside your prison at last.

6 } Take a deep breath of fresh air. Stretch out your arms. Laugh, shout, jump up and down, or express your sense of relief in any way you choose.

7 } When you're ready, open your eyes.

Do this meditation whenever you feel anxious about trying something new or making changes in your life.

DOWNLOAD KNOWLEDGE FROM YOUR HIGHER SELF

In 2007, neuroscientist Amishi Jha and Michael Baime, director of the University of Pennsylvania's Program for Stress Management, found that meditation changes the way the brain works. After meditating daily for eight weeks, research subjects showed enhanced cognitive ability, response time, and accuracy when performing challenging tests.

If you've ever found yourself in a dilemma and couldn't figure a way out, or felt paralyzed by problems that seemed overwhelming, this meditation is for you. Use it to help you see the bigger picture in a conundrum, or to discover the best course of action for all concerned. The help you need has always been there, is there now, and will always be there. It's yours for the asking.

1 } Sit or lie comfortably, with your eyes closed. Take a deep breath and exhale. Do this two more times. Relax using whichever method you prefer. After you are relaxed, mentally count down from seven to one, relaxing more deeply with each count.

2 } On the count of one, find yourself in your Safe Place. Feel the beauty, love, blessed solitude, or enchantment of this place.

3 } Now, invite your Higher Self to join you. Sit together. Talk of your dilemma, problem, or feeling of being overwhelmed. Ask for help. Ask to grow from this challenge. Ask to become more.

4 } Now, sit facing each other with legs crossed. Together, you and your Higher Self slowly bend forward and touch foreheads.

5 } Feel your Higher Self downloading all you need into your brain. This will only take a few seconds. Don't try to figure anything out or try to find answers yet. Just feel the powerful sensation of the download. When done, you and your Higher Self return to your upright sitting positions.

6 } Thank your Higher Self and allow yourself to feel gratitude. Close your mental eyes and mentally count from one to five.

7 } On the count of five, open your physical eyes and return.

The answers may not come to you right away, but they will come. They might just pop into your awareness, seemingly "out of the blue." They may come in dreams. You might find them in the most mundane or the most amazing ways. Be open to them.

GAIN ANSWERS THROUGH CONTEMPLATION

Often contemplation is associated with Zen Buddhism, but it has been a part of many spiritual practices worldwide for millennia. Contemplation involves focusing on an idea, a question, a word, or a phrase in order to gain a deeper understanding of it. According to Father Thomas Keating, founder of Contemplative Outreach, Ltd., contemplation gives us "a sense of interconnectedness with all creation." Spiritual teacher, author, artist, and composer Sri Chinmoy says, "When we are contemplating we feel that we are holding within ourselves the entire universe with all its infinite light, peace, bliss, and truth."

You needn't follow any particular religion or spiritual path to benefit from contemplation, however. At the Center for Contemplative Mind in Society, contemplation is defined simply as "the exploration of a topic or question." The following practice is one you can use to gain answers to problems or to deepen your understanding of an aspect of your life.

1 } Choose an idea, a question, or a situation about which you would like to gain greater insight and understanding. It might be a single word, such as *peace* or *abundance*. It might be a concept, such as the role of service in society. Or, it could be about a personal concern, such as why a loved one behaves in a certain way.

2 } Sit or lie comfortably, with your eyes closed. Take a deep breath and exhale three times. Relax using whichever method you prefer.

3 } Bring to mind whatever it is you wish to understand more deeply. Focus your attention on that idea. In your calm, relaxed state, allow your mind to begin exploring the idea.

4 } Start with what you know about the subject of your contemplation. Then, let your thoughts expand to encompass other aspects of the idea. Bring up memories related to the idea or question. Keep your mind relaxed, detached, and open. You'll start to receive insights or ideas concerning your idea or question that you weren't aware of before you sat down to contemplate.

5 } Attempt to see the subject of your interest from various perspectives, without judging them good or bad. If you find your thoughts spiraling too far away from the topic, stop and bring your attention to your breathing for a few moments.

6 } Then, ask your question again or refocus on your idea. Continue for as long as you like.

7 } When you feel you've gained as much insight or understanding as possible at this time, turn your attention back to your breathing. After a few breaths, open your eyes.

We've been told that the way to change the world is to find a cause, partner up with as many like-minded people as you can, then do your best to spark public awareness and pass legislation. However, it's not the only way to change the world. Each of us has the power to change anything and everything—no exceptions. As it is often said in many different ways, "Nothing changes until you do."

MEDITATIONS TO
HEAL THE
PLANET

HANG PRAYER FLAGS TO SEND BLESSINGS AROUND THE WORLD

For more than a thousand years, Tibetans have hung prayer flags inscribed with sacred symbols, prayers, and images of deities near their homes, temples, businesses, and sacred sites. According to tradition, when the flags flutter in the wind, the prayers blow around the world to bless all Earth's inhabitants.

You can make a single prayer flag or many. Traditional Tibetan prayer flags are made in five colors—red, yellow, green, blue, and white—that correspond to the five elements that Tibetans believe compose our world. However, you may choose cloth of whatever color(s) you prefer.

1 } Put aside all daily concerns and considerations, and allow yourself to relax. Cut one or more squares of colored cloth—as many as you like—each about 8 inches (20 cm) square.

2 } Using a felt marker with permanent ink, write a prayer or blessing on one piece of cloth. If you wish, add meaningful symbols or pictures that represent your intentions (e.g., a dove for peace, a heart for love, and so on). As you write, contemplate your intentions.

3 } Keep your thoughts focused on what you are writing or drawing—don't let your mind wander.

4 } When you've finished, write another prayer or blessing on a second piece of cloth. Continue writing prayers—one per flag—until you're satisfied that you've stated all your intentions.

After you've created several prayer flags, sew, pin, or otherwise attach the squares of colored cloth to a piece of string, so they look like laundry hanging on a clothesline.

5 } Take the flags outside and fasten them to your home, a tree, a fence, or another place where they can blow in the breeze. As the wind catches the flags and causes them to flutter, imagine your blessings drifting on the wind to the four corners of Earth. Imagine people, animals, plants, and other beings receiving your blessings.

6 } Imagine your prayers healing the world.

7 } When the flags have faded so they can no longer be read, take them down and create more.

THE BEST MEDITATIONS ON THE PLANET

STUDY A FLOWER TO APPRECIATE NATURE

Rudolf Steiner, who founded the Anthroposophical Society and the Waldorf Schools, recommended studying flowers as a way to expand your awareness. In *The Secret Life of Plants*, authors Peter Tompkins and Christopher Bird reported studies done by lie detector examiner Cleve Backster almost half a century ago that proved plants respond to human thoughts.

This meditative practice induces a sense of calm and balance by connecting you with the natural world. It also strengthens your own powers of observation and lets you simultaneously impact nature in a positive way.

~~~~~

1 } Select a flower, growing in a garden, a container, or in the wild. Stand, sit, or kneel in front of the flower in a way that is comfortable for you, so you can observe it closely.

2 } Put aside all thoughts and other considerations for the time being. Gaze at the flower, as if you were seeing it for the first time—in a sense, you are. Observe the color(s) and shape(s) of its petals. Notice the subtle differences from one petal to another.

3 } Examine the pistil and stamens, and the pattern they form in the center of the flower. Notice how the flower's leaves sprout from the stem, each unique from the others. Pay attention to the smallest details.

4 } Keep your attention focused on the flower. If unrelated thoughts arise into your awareness, gently ease them out of your mind and refocus your attention on the flower.

5 } Smell the flower's scent. Allow yourself to enjoy the aroma fully. Appreciate the flower's complex beauty, and the many individual features that compose its whole.

6 } Realizing that the flower is a living thing, try to sense its vital energy. You might see a faint aura around the flower or feel a slight tingling if you touch the plant.

7 } Try to make a loving connection with the flower. You may feel a bond with it, or even sense a form of communication flowing between you and the flower. Continue observing the flower for as long as you like.

Practice this meditation regularly, observing flowers and plants of various kinds. Allow your sense of awe and respect to deepen over time. You'll likely notice that spending time with flowers leaves you feeling peaceful and relaxed. By sending loving thoughts to the plants you study, you'll also help them grow stronger and healthier.

OBSERVE WATER TO PERCEIVE LIFE ENERGY

Wilhelm Reich, an Austrian-born psychologist and colleague of Freud's in the 1920s, spent his later years in the United States studying and writing about a universal life energy he referred to as *orgone*. This energy, which Chinese medicine calls *qi* or *chi*, flows through the earth and all living things. Reich found that when he focused and directed this energy on patients with arthritis, cancer, and other diseases, their health improved. His research also showed that orgone is concentrated in lakes, rivers, and waterfalls, which may be one reason we feel peaceful and refreshed when we sit beside a body of water.

1 } Sit near a lake, pond, stream, or other body of water. Relax, and gently ease all thoughts out of your mind as you gaze at the water.

2 } Instead of staring into the water, cast your gaze slightly above the water's surface.

3 } Notice a slight shimmering or bluish haze rippling just above the surface of the water.

4 } Keep watching, letting your vision relax and even blur a bit. You'll notice the bluish haze moves in a circular pattern.

5 } What you are observing is orgone, or qi. This energy is also moving through you, connecting you with everything else on Earth.

6 } As you continue gazing at the water, feel this life energy flowing in your body with each breath you take. Feel yourself becoming more calm and relaxed.

7 } Sit for as long as you like, observing this energy and feeling your connection with all life on Earth.

Sit beside a stream, a lake, or the ocean whenever possible, enjoying the refreshing, rejuvenating energy that exists in water.

RECEIVE WISDOM FROM A TREE

In many spiritual traditions, trees serve as conduits for wisdom. The Buddha is said to have gained enlightenment while sitting under the Bodhi Tree. The Tree of Life plays a central role in the Kabbalah, an ancient Jewish mystical system. The Druids considered all trees sacred. Because trees live a long time—some of the giant redwoods are believed to be two thousand years old—they bear witness to many experiences. You, too, can receive insights from trees—this meditation explains how.

~~~~~~

1 } Choose a tree with which you feel an affinity. It may be one growing in your own yard, the heart of the forest, or a city park. Sit beneath its branches, in a position that is comfortable for you.

2 } Take a deep breath and exhale. Do this two more times. Relax using whichever method you prefer. Sit for a while and simply choose to become calmer, more peaceful.

3 } Let your attention go to the tree. Gaze at its leaves, branches, and trunk. Look at the texture of the bark, the patterns its leaves make. Does it have flowers? Fruit or nuts? Observe any details you might ordinarily overlook.

4 } Listen to the wind rustling the tree's leaves. Hear the branches rub together. Are there any birds or squirrels in the tree? Touch the tree, if you like.

5 } After you've spent a few minutes getting familiar with the tree, close your eyes. Let yourself feel the tree's presence. See if you can sense the tree's energy, the life flowing in it. Allow your awareness to embrace the tree as a friend. Feel a connection between you and the tree. Send loving thoughts to the tree. Express your appreciation for its cool shade, its beauty, how it helps cleanse the air.

6 } Ask the tree to share its wisdom with you. Open your "mental ears" and listen to the tree's answer. You may get an impression of a response; a sudden thought, an emotion, or an image might pop into your awareness. Don't question or analyze your impressions; just receive them.

7 } Continue communing with the tree for as long as you like. When you feel ready, thank the tree.

8 } Open your eyes and return.

Any time you like, you can return to sit with this particular tree, or choose another one. The ancients believed that different species of trees possessed different characteristics beyond their physical properties and that trees could benefit humans in a variety of ways. Your appreciation and your loving thoughts help nourish the trees, too. You may wish to write down what you glean from your time spent communicating with trees.

TAKE A HIKE TO BOND WITH MOTHER EARTH

A walk in the woods, a hike along a mountain trail, or a stroll on the beach combines meditation with exercise, fresh air, and vitamin D from sunshine. No wonder many experts recommend walking to stay healthy. The purpose of this waking meditation, however, is to increase your awareness and serenity, not build muscle tone (although that might happen, too). Walking in nature also strengthens your bond with Mother Earth.

〰〰〰

1 } Choose a locale that you find pleasing. It could be a path through the woods, a quiet back road in the country, or even a city park. Determine a distance that's comfortable for you and safe for your fitness level. Take it easy—this is a meditation, not a forced march. Walk at a slow, regular pace. Pay attention to each step, feeling the ground beneath your feet.

2 } Set aside everyday thoughts, concerns, and worries for the time being. Breathe deeply and mindfully, filling your lungs with fresh air and expelling old, stale air from your lungs. Notice how your body shifts as you move, how your muscles work together harmoniously to propel you along.

3 } Feel the sun on your shoulders, the breeze in your hair. Feel yourself growing calmer, more peaceful, and centered with each step you take. Observe flora, fauna, rocks, and other natural features. Just observe them, without analysis or judgment.

4 } Enjoy watching birds, squirrels, and other wildlife. Notice how sunlight filters through the leaves of trees, how the grass waves in the wind, how shadows glide along the ground.

5 } Allow yourself to feel an appreciation for the beauty of nature, for all the sights, sounds, and smells around you.

6 } Feel your heart opening to experience a loving bond with Mother Earth and all the inhabitants who share the planet with you.

7 } Imagine that love flowing out from your heart, spreading across the land and around the world. Continue walking for as long as is comfortable for you.

Walk as often as you like, for as long as you like. Spend at least ten minutes a day, if possible; work up to longer periods when you feel ready and weather permits. You may notice a welling up of insight, inspiration, or creativity, and might want to jot down what you experience. Take walks in different locales, or follow the same route every day —but try to see your surroundings with new eyes each time.

REDUCE CONFLICT AND CRIME

In June and July of 1993, 4,000 experienced Transcendental Meditation practitioners from eighty-one countries gathered in Washington, D.C., to undertake an unusual experiment. The group's goal was to reduce violent crime by meditating. During the eight-week period, the rate of assaults, murders, rapes, and other violent crimes decreased by 23 percent. The statistical odds of this happening purely by chance was less than two in one billion, as reported in Springer Science & Business Media's journal *Social Indicators Research*.

Conflict and violent crime often are reactions to feelings of being "attacked." In many cases, however, we need not respond to an affront with aggression. This meditation helps you avoid reacting to angry words and perceived insults, thus defusing a hostile situation.

~~~~~~

1 } If someone assaults you with harsh or angry words, take a few deep breaths. Imagine your body is made of smoke.

2 } Feel yourself becoming less substantial, lighter, and freer. Keep breathing slowly and deeply.

3 } Now, imagine the other person's words as arrows coming at you.

4 } When the arrows reach you, they find no place to lodge and pass harmlessly through the smoke.

5 } You feel no need to react, because the other person's words have no impact on you. They can't hurt you.

6 } Remain in this detached state for as long as necessary. Nothing the other person says can affect you.

7 } When the other person realizes you won't respond or escalate the hostility, he or she will most likely give up.

Do this meditation whenever you feel attacked by someone else's angry words or judgments, or when you feel tempted to escalate an argument.

REDUCE NATURAL DISASTERS AND WORLD TENSION

The causes of natural disasters on our planet are a subject of scientific discussion and debate beyond the purview of this book. But one particular metaphysical explanation, although it could seem a bit "far out" for some, may help us understand the power and global magnitude of the following meditation and the profound benefits experienced by those who do it.

Some metaphysicians suggest that Earth possesses a natural electromagnetic energy. When man-made tensions and disharmony build in certain areas of the world, a kind of reversed "greenhouse effect" occurs, blocking this vital and beneficial natural energy from being absorbed and utilized within that region. As a result, a disharmonious imbalance results, producing chaotic, nonintegrated energy. This whirlwind of built-up chaotic pressure can, they claim, produce catastrophic natural occurrences. When a person, or persons, allows this energy in, natural disasters and even regional tensions either dissolve altogether or are greatly mitigated. It does not matter how far away it is occurring from you.

This energy is highly beneficial. When absorbed by living things, it produces balance and healing. When people allow this energy in, they experience great vitality, creativity, and imagination as well as improved health and well-being. You could say the experience is quite a "rush." This natural electromagnetic energy should not be confused with the highly dangerous and life-damaging man-made electromagnetic variety.

The following is a remarkably powerful meditation taught by Lazaris. Lazaris is channeled through Jach Pursel. (For more information about Lazaris and the Lazaris material, go to www.lazaris.com.)

~~~~~~

1 } Sit quietly and close your eyes.

2 } Imagine a large funnel at the crown of your head.

3 } Bring your attention to the area or region of natural turmoil or man-made conflict and tension. Maybe your attention goes to a hurricane or an earthquake forming or occurring somewhere in the world. Maybe your attention goes to some global hotbed.

4 } Imagine a massive swirl of energy whirling above that area.

5 } With your intention, draw the energy from that area or region to you. Sense it entering down into you through the funnel. Feel the energy flowing into every part of your body.

6 } Feel that energy within you, filling you, nurturing you. Feel every cell and atom being charged and fed by this energy. Feel lightness and creativity flowing. If you have a health issue, send the energy around and into the malady.

Feel it absorbing and lifting that problem. Feel the power of Earth's love. Words may not fully express the wonderful feeling you feel when allowing this energy in.

7 } Do this meditation for about ten minutes.

8 } When you are done, open your eyes and enjoy.

Check your newspaper or news stations for reports of change in the natural event, or a lessening of tensions in the area of conflict.

SEED THE PLANET WITH LOVE

When you bring more love into your life, the world becomes more loving. When you heal yourself, the world becomes more healed. You can choose to actively engage the world or sit in meditation: it doesn't matter. The world will be a better place because of who you are, not what you do. The following meditation encourages positive growth in your world. It may seem simple, but do not let its simplicity fool you.

~~~~~~~

1 } Sit or lie comfortably, with your eyes closed. Take a deep breath and exhale. Do this two more times. Relax using whichever method you prefer. After you are relaxed, mentally count down from seven to one, relaxing more deeply with each count.

2 } On the count of one, find yourself in your Safe Place. Feel the beauty, love, blessed solitude, or enchantment of this place. Invite your Higher Self to join you. Sit together.

3 } Talk of the wonderful experiences and feelings you have allowed into your life. Forget the humility—celebrate your successes. Share it with your Higher Self. When you are done, your Higher Self draws a mist or fog into this place. It becomes so thick you cannot see anything around you. Your Higher Self takes you gently by the hand and guides you through the mist/fog.

4 } When you reach the far side of the mist/fog, and it gradually drifts away, you find yourself standing with your Higher Self on a high, grassy mound at night. Feel the silence, the beauty, the majesty of this place. Now, bring up the wonderful feelings inside you. Bring up your victory, your success, your healing. Fill yourself with it.

5 } When you are completely filled to overflowing, let these joyful feelings burst out of you, like seeds from a seedpod. See or sense yourself sending out tiny seeds of light—millions and millions of seeds of happiness, joy, success, healing, abundance, and so on. Don't worry—you aren't losing it; you are sharing it.

6 } See these millions of sparkling seeds of light floating higher and higher. See them being carried by the wind to all parts of the world, to the regions of conflict and tension, to the places of poverty and despair, to the areas that need them most. When you are finished, thank your Higher Self.

7 } Close your mental eyes and mentally count from one to five. On the count of five, open your physical eyes and return to a world blessed by your love.

Do this meditation when you feel happiness, love, or another positive emotion. Know that the "seeds" you send out will settle, germinate, and grow strong. They will change the world. You have changed the world.

CO-CREATE YOUR MAGICAL GARDEN

In 1962, Peter and Eileen Caddy and Dorothy Maclean began the Findhorn Foundation in northeast Scotland. Although the soil was poor and the climate harsh, they managed to grow abundant gardens with flowers, herbs, and amazingly large vegetables. Their secret? During meditation, Dorothy received insight that they should cooperate with the nature spirits, or *devas*. They did, and their now-legendary gardens prospered, astounding horticulturists.

Deva is a Sanskrit word that means "shining one." In the natural world, devas are nonphysical beings who are responsible for the growth, maintenance, nurturance, and evolution of plants and animals. In her book *Behaving as If the God in All Life Mattered*, Machaelle Small Wright discusses the mutually beneficial outcomes that result from working *with* nature, rather than demanding that nature work *for* us. Are you a gardener, an agricultural farmer, or just interested in being closer to nature? Like Findhorn's founders, you, too, can work with the devas in a co-creative partnership to grow hardier and healthier plants, increase toxic-free crop yields, and live in harmony with the earth. The following meditation shows you how.

~~~~~~

1 } Sit or lie comfortably, with your eyes closed. Take a deep breath and exhale. Do this two more times. Relax using whichever method you prefer. After you are relaxed, mentally count down from seven to one, relaxing more deeply with each count.

2 } On the count of one, find yourself in your garden, in the open fields of your farm, or in the groves of your orchard. (You may actually meditate outdoors in your garden if you like.)

3 } Feel the beauty, the abundance, the fertile potential and richness of this place. Feel its life, its essence, its majesty. Invite the garden's deva to join you. In time, a being of light will appear—it usually looks like a sparkle of luminescent light. Sense its grandeur, its love, its

magnificence. Speak to this deva of your desire to co-create with this place. Conclude with, "I desire this co-creation for the highest good of all and with harm to none."

4 } If the deva agrees, thank it. (If the deva does not agree, thank it as well. Its lack of agreement does not mean you are wrong, only that you need to be more willing to accept nature's guidance first.) Communicate with the deva, perhaps in words or pictures. You may even experience a form of telepathy.

5 } Ask what to plant, how the plants should be arranged, what's best to place on or near the plants to help their growth. Discuss everything. You may find that the roses don't want to be near the fence—maybe they'd rather be by the

fountain. Maybe there's too much moisture in a particular location, and the peas would be happier next to the lettuce.

6 } Even if it goes against everything you've learned, or what the "experts" told you, follow the deva's advice. Find out what's necessary to bring about a win/win situation for all. When you've finished, the deva will disappear.

7 } Now close your mental eyes and mentally count from one to five. On the count of five, open your physical eyes and return.

Spend as long as you like communicating with the deva. If you don't experience any form of communication, try using the automatic writing technique "Unblock Your Creativity" in part 10. Repeat this meditation often to ensure your garden's health, fertility, and abundance.

MORE ABOUT MEDITATION

Meditation's Spiritual Roots

Five thousand years ago, the authors of the Hindu sacred texts known as the Vedas recorded the first written discussions of meditation practices. According to the Rig Veda, meditation's purpose is to "manifest the Sun," meaning to gain expanded consciousness or enlightenment. Part of Vedic meditation involves the repetition of a mantra, a sacred utterance that guides the mind toward higher realities.

About 2,500 years later, the Hindu prince Siddhartha Gautama, while meditating beneath the Bodhi Tree, realized enlightenment and became a Buddha. He spent the rest of his life teaching the practice of meditation as part of the spiritual path he had discovered. One category of Buddhist meditation known as *vipassana*, meaning "insight," emphasizes quieting the mind, opening the heart, and transcending the sense of ego-separateness that causes suffering. In Zen meditation, which is influenced by both Buddhist and Taoist thought, the objective is to keep the mind present in the moment. Contemplating koans (puzzles without answers) and waking mindfulness techniques, such as raking a garden or creating mandalas, are sometimes employed for this purpose.

Although we usually associate meditation with Eastern spirituality, virtually all the major world religions have advocated some type of meditation. Both the Old and the New Testaments discuss meditation. *Lectio divina*, which involves meditation along with prayer, contemplation, and reading, has been practiced since the fourth century. Thomas Merton, a twentieth-century Catholic monk who studied Eastern meditation techniques, revived interest in Christian meditation and contemplation during the past fifty years. Merton explained meditation as a "prayer of the heart" with no words or thoughts.

In the Jewish religion, meditation involves cultivating awareness of a divine presence, as well as developing the qualities of wisdom and compassion. Kabbalah, an ancient Jewish mystical system that is part of the Torah, includes meditation on the Tree of Life and other symbols as a means to directly interact with the higher worlds. In Islam, meditation based on contemplation is called *tafakkur*, a form of reflection upon the universe to receive divine inspiration. Meditation is also part of the Sufi Way, a mystical branch of Islam.

The mystery schools of ancient Egypt, Greece, and Rome taught meditation. Native American tribes as well as indigenous Pagan populations practiced it. Some researchers even trace meditation back to the Stone Age, pointing to cave paintings that depict people in trancelike states as evidence.

However, you needn't adhere to any particular spiritual path, belief system, or cultural background in order to meditate and reap the benefits. Meditation's universality and long history clearly show that it can be enjoyed by anyone, anywhere, anytime. In fact, most people today choose meditation for practical reasons: relaxation, physical and emotional healing, improved mental abilities, and a better quality of life—the very things we cover in this book.

Directed and Nondirected Meditations

Meditation comes in many flavors—you can find many hundreds of types of meditations and styles of meditating. All cultures, all traditions, and all

major religions incorporate some type of meditation into their beliefs and rituals. Meditations can include singing, chanting, dancing, prayer, contemplation, or some austere practices. But all meditations fall into one of two basic categories: directed and nondirected.

Directed meditations are those in which you "direct" your mind to subtle inward or outward experiences using feeling and imagination. You may seek to gain access to subconscious or unconscious information, or to explore subconscious or unconscious experiences using a process of "inner journeying"—a form of directed inward meditation. Intentionally altering your consciousness while in a waking or active state in order to produce greater receptivity, understanding, synchronicity, and connection with your inner self and everything around you is a form of directed outward meditation. Sometimes referred to as "waking meditations," these altered states of consciousness include such practices as walking a labyrinth, raking a Zen garden, and yoga.

Nondirected meditations are usually inward experiences intended to elevate you to higher states of consciousness. These meditations are designed to let you manage the thinking process (mindfulness meditation) or transcend thinking altogether (Transcendental Meditation technique). Directed meditation honors and utilizes thoughts; nondirected meditation does not.

Most of the meditations contained in this book are directed meditations. Some are inward, some are outward (waking) meditations. Both activate higher states of consciousness and connect you with deeper parts of yourself as well as with All That Is. We do not address the Transcendental Meditation technique here because it can only be learned properly from a trained TM teacher, not from reading a book. We prefer directed meditations in most instances because they produce profound results elegantly and immediately. More important, they invite you to become a conscious participant and cocreator in your own growth, healing, and change. In nondirected meditation, you are a passive recipient of insight, healing, and elevated consciousness.

Some Types of Meditation

The best-known form of meditation is Transcendental Meditation (TM), which an estimated one million Americans practice regularly. This nondirected meditative technique involves transcending the thinking process through the use of a specifically selected mantra to provide deep mental and physical relaxation, stress release, and higher states of consciousness.

In mindfulness or insight meditation, another type of nondirected meditation believed to have been taught by Gautama Buddha 2,500 years ago, you pay attention to your breathing. When thoughts or emotions arise, you simply acknowledge them and let them go, without judgment or analysis.

Contemplation (reflection) involves focusing on a particular object, idea, or image to gain greater insight into it. Reflecting on Zen koans—ideas that can't be understood through logic or rational thinking—falls into this category. An example would be to meditate on the phrase "What is the sound of one hand clapping?"

In creative visualization, you form a mental picture that conveys relaxation, such as waves breaking gently on the sand, or a scenario that helps you work on specific conditions through using your imagination.

Active (waking) meditation sounds like an oxymoron, but that's exactly what you're doing when you stroll peacefully through the woods or walk a labyrinth. The key is to move slowly and mindfully, remaining attentive to your motions.

CROSS-REFERENCE CHART

In this section, we've listed various meditations we feel can aid particular conditions and objectives. However, as we said in part 1, the meditations contained in this book are versatile and can be adapted to address your specific needs or desires. We urge you to work with them, experiment, and find the ones that suit you best.

HEALTH (PHYSICAL)

HEALTH (EMOTIONAL)

MENTAL ABILITY, LEARNING, AND EDUCATION

CREATIVITY

SUCCESS

SPORTS/FITNESS

RELATIONSHIPS

HEALING THE PLANET

CONNECTING WITH NATURE

HANDLING NATURAL DISASTERS

PEACE

RELIEVING GLOBAL CRISIS/TENSIONS

ACKNOWLEDGMENTS

We'd like to thank the following for their assistance in bringing this book into being: Rho, friend and counselor, channeled through Debra Franco; Lazaris, channeled through Jach Pursel, a friend in whose guidance amazing journeys are taken, and from whose wisdom and love, life-changing experiences happen; teachers Hal Robinson and Willie McDaniel; and the Fair Winds Press staff, especially Jill Alexander, who believed in this book from the beginning.

ABOUT THE AUTHORS

DR. MARTIN HART is the founder and president of the American Society of Alternative Therapists (ASAT™) and has been in private counseling and alternative health education for more than thirty-five years. Since 1978, Dr. Hart has conducted workshops and lectures throughout the United States and the world on meditation and other life-enhancing subjects. He has taught at some of the largest corporations in Asia, as well as top colleges and research facilities. In the late 1980s, he incorporated a series of unique healing modalities based on his successful counseling practice into a healing concept called ASAT C.O.R.E. Counseling, which, among other things, incorporates specifically designed meditations into a highly effective counseling approach. "Through ASAT™ C.O.R.E. Counseling, my students and I have seen the lives of thousands of our clients blossom and grow in remarkable ways. They are crafting exceptional lives that are fun, empowering, and even magical. Where struggle and conflict once flourished in their lives, now challenge and elegance thrive. And all this has happened in a remarkably short period of time. Our clients report being happier, healthier, more successful, and more productive, and their lives are taking on a kind of magic marked by glorious synchronicities." As a result of the efficacy of this approach, Dr. Hart started training ASAT C.O.R.E. counselors in 1990 through live trainings and home study. There are now more than 1,700 certified ASAT C.O.R.E counselors throughout the world. Dr. Hart still travels the United States and the world, conducting his trainings as well as other related lectures and workshops. His courses and workshops have been featured in the *Wall Street Journal, Boston Globe, London Sunday Telegraph*, and other publications. He has also appeared on national and international television and radio programs discussing his unique work. To contact him regarding his trainings and workshops, send an email to asat@asat.org or visit ASAT's website at www.asat.org.

SKYE ALEXANDER is the author of more than thirty books and healing card decks, including *The Pocket Encyclopedia of Healing Touch Therapies*, *10-Minute Feng Shui,* and *The Care and Feeding of Your Chi*. Meditation and yoga have been part of her daily regimen for thirty-five years. You can visit her website and blog at www.skyealexander.com.